What people say

Susan's
Positive Parenting Plan

"I TOOK SUSAN'S PARENTING CLASS in desperation when my sons were 7 and 5 years old. My youngest acted out all the time and was rude and uncooperative. The class taught me to set limits and stick to them, disengage from power struggles and establish family meeting times so we all could express ourselves. Learning

Susan's positive parenting plan helped our family to get along better, respect each other more, and enjoy family life. Today my sons are happy, independent adults whose company my husband and I enjoy. They mean it when they tell us they're glad about the way they were raised."

DENALI DELMAR, WESTFORD, MASS.

"SUSAN'S WORKSHOPS showed our family the value of family meetings. All six of us gathered every Sunday night for as long as an hour to talk about the highs and lows of our week, plan dinner menus, divide up chores, and get to know each other better. Even the youngest had chores that her older siblings taught her how to do. The meetings gave our family a regular time to slow down and connect."

BARBARA CALDWELL-MILLER, LITTLETON, MASS.

What people say
Susan's
Positive Parenting Plan

"SUSAN'S POSITIVE PARENTING PLAN reminded me to take better care of myself and my marriage. I climbed out my funk, and our family is stronger. She taught me to set kind and firm limits with the children. Susan's down-to-earth advice makes my days easier. I have more energy to welcome our third child into the world."

BERNADETT CAMPBELL, STONEHAM, MASS.

"WHEN MY 2-YEAR-OLD REFUSED to stay in bed at night I lost sleep and worried about his safety. Reasoning, bribery and being very stern failed. Nothing worked until Susan gave me 'permission' to close the door."

D.F., WESTFORD, MASS.

"WHEN SUSAN INVITED US TO BRING unfinished craft projects to class to practice encouraging each other for our efforts, it showed me the importance of not only encouraging our children, but of self-encouragement.
Learning how to encourage has given me courage to try new things and be a lifelong learner."

K.S, WESTFORD, MASS.

RAISING
ABLE

How chores cultivate capable confident young people

By Susan Tordella

Black Eyed Susan Publications
Boston

Raising Able: How chores cultivate capable confident young people
By Susan Tordella

Black Eyed Susan Publications
www.raisingable.com, telephone 978-846-2811

ISBN: 978-0-9826973-0-6

Table of contents

*The key is changing our habits, and in particular,
the habits of our mind.*
Pema Chödrön

Preface

My approach to parenting changed radically after one lazy August afternoon at the community swimming pool when I angrily gave Ian, 21 months, a "time out" in a corner of the chain link fence around the pool while Jamie Bafundo watched.

"I told you to leave Noah alone!" I said, and led Ian to a corner for trying to take Noah's float again. I believed that making Ian suffer for antagonizing his brother was the only way he would learn to behave.

Sound familiar?

Jamie observed the scenario without comment. I didn't know her well. We started chatting. After a few minutes she said, "Why don't you come to a parenting class in September? It has helped me be a better mother."

"I don't want to go to a gripe session."

"It's not that. We read a book together and talk about it. I've learned to deal with my children without yelling," Jamie said.

That was a selling point. The youngest three of Jamie's five children played peacefully in the same baby pool where mine were fighting. The group would be led by a mother, not an "expert" who had never been with children for extended time.

"We'll have a babysitter at the church to take care of the children during class. We pitch in to pay her," Jamie said.

Now we were talking. At the very least, I'd have a break from my gang of three, and hopefully learn something.

"Okay. How do I sign up?" I said.

Jamie Bafundo and the Family Education Center of Delaware introduced me to one consistent positive parenting plan that transformed our family, and provided a foundation for nearly thirty years of parenting.

Based on the psychology of Alfred Adler, M.D., the approach shepherded me through thirteen years of sharing my home and car with my four teens and two teenage exchange students.

The Adlerian way became my rudder. I didn't have to blow in the wind with the latest parenting trends.

Alfred Adler was a contemporary of Sigmund Freud and Carl Jung, all members of Freud's famous Wednesday Group that founded modern psychiatry in the early 1900s. Adler's psychology is based on the idea the primary need of humans is to belong to a social group. He introduced the concepts of birth order and natural and logical consequences instead of punishment and reward.

His protégé, Rudolf Dreikurs, M.D., translated Adler's theory into practice and formed parenting centers. Dreikurs published the seminal book, *Children: the Challenge* in 1964 with co-author Vicki Soltz. While a bit dated, families today face similar problems. The authors offer insightful analysis of situations and useful suggestions a

I began taking an eight-week study group in the fall and spring, and sometimes one in the summer. After a few years, I learned enough from my mistakes and successes to start co-leading parenting workshops. I like to joke, "I taught what I most needed to learn."

Our family moved to the Boston area in 1990. I began offering parenting skills workshops at a community center in my town. Parents join group to learn a new approach to one of life's most difficult and rewarding tasks.

Some people sign up because they came from a dysfunctional family and wanted to learn a positive parenting approach that they had never experienced.

For example, a participant said, "My parents were both alcoholics. We were left to grow up on our own. I'm lucky I turned out as normally as I did. We want to do something different for our children, but don't have a clue what a normal family is."

Her husband, Bill, an entrepreneur, set aside Tuesday mornings for eight weeks to learn a positive parenting plan because he said, "My childhood was just as chaotic."

Other parents come to the workshops because they realize what they are doing isn't working. Participants who are the most frustrated and ready to give up are often the best students because they implement the new strategies without question and complete conviction.

Each time I took and taught a workshop, a different aspect of the system intrigued me and I decided, "That's the key."

My first insight came early when I realized that I was in a power struggle with my oldest daughter, Casey, 6 years old at the time. I learned to avoid the power dance and my home and my heart became calmer.

Casey and I are *still* two Alpha women who occasionally tussle for power. Learning the mistaken goals of misbehavior (see Chapter 17, *Name it and Tame It*) allowed me to identify what the children and I were thinking and feeling, for me be accountable to my role in the conflict, and to have a positive parenting plan ready to respond differently.

Tweaking my response created a cause-and-effect. My family changed dramatically as I began incorporating family meetings, encouragement, and gave up punishment and reward in favor of natural and logical consequences. I had a plan and it worked.

Join a study group or online community

The only way I've ever significantly changed my thoughts, feelings and deeds has been by sitting in a circle with people who shared the same pain and wanted relief. We met weekly for two or three months, studied and discussed how to change. We practiced the theory in between sessions – until we internalized the lessons.

We shared our doubts and failures. The teacher taught us new strategies, which we applied to our families and lives for a week. We returned to the hive for another bite of honey, support, laughter, to share stories on our mistakes and successes, and the courage to try again. After much practice, I became a teacher.

You will benefit from reading the book alone. Joining a study group will magnify the results ten times. The results will be more memorable by studying it with other parents, ideally with friends and your spouse. A united team is much more likely to succeed. Participating in an online community can be as effective as a face-to-face group.

Blended families especially benefit from adopting one unified approach. However, if your spouse, former spouse or significant other does not embrace the new plan, one parent can implement it unilaterally. A change in your child's behavior may convince other adults to follow suit. If not, don't worry about it. Children are perceptive and adaptable.

Every group I participated in allowed me to polish my skills, gain confidence and have a happier heart and home. I experienced results immediately and built on success. In between courses, I started to slide back to my old ways of yelling, threatening and losing patience. Another class and a different Adlerian-based book reminded me of the power of a positive parenting plan.

It took about three years to train myself to automatically respond differently, to give up almost all of the yelling and anger, replace reward and punishment with encouragement, family meetings and natural and logical consequences.

I changed and our family atmosphere changed.

Disciplining – teaching – our oldest three children became less stressful and easier when I had a positive parenting plan. After a year, using the new strategies gave me the courage to have a fourth child. I'm not advocating for bigger families, just more harmonious ones.

My husband Bob and I laid a foundation during the first twelve years that made the next thirteen years of raising teenagers tolerable, even enjoyable. This book will benefit parents of tots-to-teens.

60 miles away going 60 miles an hour

Thanks to chores and the Adlerian approach, my children evolved into teenagers who made good independent decisions when they were 60 miles away going 60 miles an hour. Now in their twenties, they ably manage their money, time, careers, education and relationships.

Even though they were raised in a fairly affluent community, they managed to avoid the entitlement trap. **It's impossible to feel entitled when you clean toilets, pick up dog manure and wash dishes.**

These humble activities teach valuable lifelong lessons. Doing chores impacts young people on the soul level, while contributing to the good of the family and easing the burden on parents.

I surveyed 560 people between ages 11 and 92 about childhood chores and the respondents affirmed that chores teach responsibility and teamwork.

Doing a few chores regularly is a powerful teaching tool when combined with the rest of the Adlerian approach. When children pitch in, parents can retire from being the house servant. You will feel better, your home and yard will be better maintained, and your children will hopefully make better decisions.

The power of stories

Stories are powerful teaching tools. When we see ourselves as characters in the stories it makes learning more interesting than studying theory. I've collected many stories for your reading and learning pleasure.

The stories in this book come from many sources. Many names have been changed to protect people's identities. A few stories contain a synthesis of characters to illustrate a concept. The stories about our family are true, warts and all, and approved by my children. My many mistakes provide excellent illustrations.

People who contributed stories about how childhood chores impacted them for life are cited by name, and in some cases, their website and business name.

The more extreme the story, the more interesting and memorable, and the more likely we learn from them. I look forward to hearing your stories on my blog, www.raisingable.com

Being a mother has been my greatest joy and challenge in life. This book is to ease your journey, give you confidence, and to *prepare* for the teen years, not *despair* about them.

Confucius says, "The journey of a thousand miles begins with a single step." Let's get going.

You know the only people who are always sure about the proper way to raise children? Those who've never had any.
Bill Cosby

1
A Positive Parenting Plan

The gray hue on the thirty-five windows of our house cast pallor on the sunniest days, so I called an informal family meeting in the middle of spring break.

"We're going to clean the windows together today and one of you can clean four carpets."

Casey, 16, and Noah, 14, immediately and emphatically said, "No!" Ian, 12, and Kristen, 9, said nothing.

"You need to adjust your attitude towards work," I said.

All four of them regularly did dishes, mowed the lawn, helped with cooking, and cleaned house. All I wanted was four hours or so of focused labor. Five times four equaled twenty hours of work and clean windows and carpets.

"I'll clean the rugs," Casey volunteered, and set off to set up the shampooer. Choosing one's task gives a modicum of control, and she, like me, enjoys being in control. With her working independently, that left two teams of four and reduced the potential for conflict.

Noah and Ian started on the second floor windows using the extension ladder. The challenge of being perched twenty feet up thrilled them and terrorized me. When I helped Ian moved the ladder to the second window, it teetered and crashed to the ground. We jumped out of the way, relieved to be safe.

"Watch out! You have to be more careful. Hold it straight upright while we're moving it!" I said, my voice thick with worry and angst.

"Mom, you need to adjust your attitude," said Ian. Noah chimed in from the window above.

I realized the gangly ladder was difficult to control. The crash provided a warning. Humbly, I adjusted my attitude.

Kristen and I made a good team. She was young enough to get lost in the Zen of the task. She reminded me to be present in the squirting, wiping and appreciating the results. Her cleaning endurance was not as magnanimous as her disposition. She washed quite a few windows for her age with the fewest complaints and least conflict. She liked being part of the team.

I enjoyed working with her, between interruptions.

When cleaning the living room windows, we saw stuffed animals raining down outside from her bedroom above. Mock screams could be heard.

"They're throwing my stuffed animals out the window!" Kristen yelled as we ran upstairs to halt the havoc. I stifled a smile and gently reprimanded the boys.

Back to work. The boys and I gingerly moved the precarious ladder to the five high windows out back. It felt like a circus balancing act. Secretly, I was glad they were willing to work on the ladder, a benign way to flex testosterone and take risks, essential in their transition from boy to man.

Kristen and I moved to the dining room. I went upstairs to check on Casey's progress on the carpets and something caught my eye in the bathroom.

Ian was squirting the water pic at Noah, perched on the ladder outside, two stories up. I put a stop to Ian's assault and gave another safety lecture. They were pushing the limits. I kept the lecture short, stern and to the point. A fall from twenty-five feet up could be devastating. They brushed me off, believing as teens do, that they're immortal.

Casey made steady, solo peaceful progress on the carpets.

We broke for lunch, barely halfway done. Over the years, the children taught me to take frequent breaks to recharge. More breaks meant more time to finish, however, more breaks might give them more energy to work longer. Emphasis on *might*. Outnumbered, I surrendered to their pace. We cranked up the stereo and went back to work.

Kristen and I were in the front of the house when the sound of breaking glass pierced the air. It sounded like a picture window shattered. I dashed into the kitchen where the extension ladder had pierced two small window panes and thought, *perhaps I expected too much from them to handle the extension ladder.*

No one was hurt. Bob could easily repair the windows on Saturday. He was at work and escaped the tumult of window-washing.

I began to wear out and wondered how much a professional window washing service would have cost. We finished the windows, which were fairly clean, and put everything away. I pulled some leftovers from the freezer for dinner and collapsed. It was several years before I could find the strength, time and energy for a family window cleaning day.

The risks and rewards of cleaning windows

You may be thinking, "Was it worth it?"

I was optimistic, young, on a budget and motivated to involve them in housework. The children were playful, thrill-seeking and capable. They learned about collaboration, a work ethic, cleaning, and how to use an extension ladder. I pushed the limits of child labor. Bob would have made a big difference. He could handle the extension ladder and would have provided more supervision. I was reluctant to use a precious Saturday to clean windows. So I took on the project alone to reinforce our family values of having fun while working together and saving money.

We often transmitted those values without taking on the ambitious project of cleaning thirty-five windows. The simple act of the children doing dishes nightly -- whether they felt like it or not -- taught self-discipline and reminded them we depend on their contributions.

Taking responsibility for chores overflowed into other areas of their lives almost immediately. The children had the self-discipline to manage their school work from elementary school onwards. They were in charge of practicing their instruments, keeping track of library books, and doing their laundry starting at age 10 or 12.

At 15, Casey got hired at Boston Market. When Noah followed in her footsteps, they gained a reputation for being good workers. Ian came next. Ian, now 25, said, "When I was growing up, I knew other children didn't have to do the dishes or pack their own lunch, and I resented it.

"At 14, I got a job at Boston Market where my older brother and sister worked. I found out that our family was known for being excellent workers and realized my mother wasn't just torturing us. There are dishes that need doing, and everyone should do them. Chores taught me to be self-reliant. Many of my friends are now learning skills I learned when I was 8."

Their work ethic was basic: show up on time, follow directions and get along with crew and customers. Those simple attributes have served them well through elementary, middle and high school, college and into their careers.

A simple routine of a few childhood chores teaches valuable life lessons. The chores do not have to be as complex as washing thirty-five windows. The children must be held accountable to complete the jobs by an agreed upon time. Most of the chores must be for the common good. No money changes hands, unless the children pay parents for what we for them.

How to get started

When I announced the window project, my teens said, "No!"

A different approach would have been to say in advance, "The windows need cleaning. I need your help. What day during vacation week would be best for you to help?" Such a request shows mutual respect, a building block to inviting children to contribute. Finesse is required to involve children with housework. A holistic positive parenting plan will grease the wheels and make it easier to involve children in chores.

The goal of this book is to set up a positive parenting plan that uses chores, encouragement, mutual respect, family meetings, and natural and logical consequences.

This positive parenting plan will:
1. Enhance the harmony in your home and prevent entitlement;
2. Involve children from a very young age to share in the work of running a household so you can retire from being the house servant;

3. Grow children into teenagers who will make good decisions when they're 60 miles away going 60 miles an hour.

I judge success by the third goal, to nurture children to make good independent decisions. Three times a shaky voice on the other end of the phone has said, "I've had an accident. Can you come and get me?"

They each unbuckled their seatbelt and walked away from the crumpled cars, sober, when they were 60 miles away, going 60 miles an hour.

Accidents happen. Teens make not-so-great decisions all the time. Readers, plead the Fifth Amendment about your adolescence.

Hopefully, teens survive and learn from their decisions and the good decisions outweigh the not-so-good decisions.

Ideally, by age 11 or 12, tweens will internalize your values. By the time they're teens, you can count on them to make good decisions when they're driving 60 miles an hour and you're 60 miles away.

This book is intended for parents of tots-to-teens. The sooner you establish a positive parenting plan, the easier you will sail through adolescence – and have skill to navigate in rough waters.

Computer commodore for life

I really wanted a Commodore 64 computer when I was 12 years old in 1982.

My dad made me a deal: he would buy the computer if I promised to help him print mailing and address labels. He bought it. I worked for my dad for three years and learned how to program the computer.

If it wasn't for my dad making me generate labels (he sells insurance and is a financial planner), my life would be remarkably different.

At 16, I started a successful Internet technology consulting business that I run today, now called Brainlink.

My father launched my career, and life-long passion with that simple request.

Rajesh Goel   Queens, New York
Chief Technology Officer--www.brainlink.com

Highlights of a positive parenting plan

Here's an outline of the positive parenting practices in this book so parents can retire as the live-in servants, and counteract entitlement.

- Set a limit, give one kind and firm warning, and then take action. Implement this one practice and it will transform your children's behavior and family environment.
- Hold family meetings two to four times a month to determine together children's contribution to the household. Children as young as 3 and 4 years old can attend family meetings. Even 2 year olds can take responsibility for small jobs.
- Follow through to make sure children and teens did what they said they going to do, when they said they would. Be diligent if you want results and choose your battles.
- Do not pay children for doing chores unless they start paying you for everything you do and provide.
- Pay children a weekly allowance not related to chores. Expect them to budget it to last the week. Model how to manage money and *affluenza* (a consuming desire for more possessions).
- Prepare and eat a family meal together three or more times a week. Turn off the TV, ban electronics and talk with each other.
- Practice the art of encouragement instead of praise. This is the heart and soul of setting up a positive relationship with your children. Become an encouragement connoisseur.
- Use natural and logical consequences instead of punishment of reward, unless you like power struggles, revenge and resentment.
- Allow yourself the courage to be imperfect and to learn from your mistakes.
- Learn Adler's theory of why children misbehave and apply it to your tots-to-teens. See Chapter 17, *Name it and Tame it.*

The goal is to shepherd children through a calm adolescence to finish high school, technical training or college, have the skills and discipline to live independently, hold down a job and form enduring relationships.

To reach the goal, allow them to make small decisions during the first decade so they will make good decisions later when you're not around.

The practices are simple and the household jobs are easy to incorporate. Start with small steps and think big. Have faith even when your children push back and protest saying, "I am not your servant!" Nor are you theirs.

The meaning of *discipline*

The Latin origin of discipline is *disciple*, meaning student. The modern definition of discipline has been misinterpreted as *punishment*. This positive parenting plan advocates that children learn better through encouragement, natural and logical consequences, family meetings, chores and mutual respect rather than punishment.

As parents, our job is to teach children. Punishment is often irrelevant, unnecessary and harsh. Youngsters usually suffer enough when they make a bad decision.

When I make a bad decision, the accompanying pain reminds me to change my behavior without someone hounding me. Children can learn without being punished, overpowered, grounded, physically harmed, blamed or shamed.

One of my favorite bad examples of teaching children is when a mom (or dad) watches William, 4, hit his sister, 2. Mom grabs William, hits him and yells, "Don't ever hit your sister again!" It's an ironic example of what not to do.

Recall the best teacher you ever had – inside or outside of school. That person probably didn't hit, belittle or threaten you to make a point. Your best teacher probably made learning fun, encouraged you to believe in yourself, challenged you to take risks, celebrated your accomplishments, and consoled you after setbacks.

Parents are tasked with being an ideal teacher by example, usually based on how we were raised. Unfortunately, we're human, and therefore imperfect. We make mistakes, lose patience, and sometimes just don't feel like being an ideal teacher in every moment.

Lucky for us, our children forgive us for not being perfect. Lucky for us, every day is a new day when and we can try again.

Learning to be a *good enough* parent and developing patience will spill over into life outside of the family. Raising children is a course in self-development. Parents encounter the extremes of the emotional spectrum. I feel a deeper love towards my children than I ever knew existed. With that love and responsibility comes a range of emotions from love to hate, patience to anger and understanding to frustration.

That range of emotion taught me to have what Dreikurs calls "the courage to be imperfect." Parenting is the toughest job you will ever love. It takes courage to stick with it.

Act, don't talk

A key aspect of a positive parenting plan is to **say what you mean and mean what you say.** Actions speak louder than words.

Give one firm warning in a friendly voice, and then take action, immediately and without rancor. No exceptions.

Children don't reach the age of reason until age 7, so don't waste your breath reasoning with little ones.

Give up counting to three, bribery, threats, cajoling, multiple warnings, and reasoning. Instead, be quiet and move.

Taking action:

- eliminates "mother deafness," when parents have trained children to ignore counting to three, bribery, threats, cajoling, warnings, and reasoning;
- eliminates parental anger that comes from feeling out-of-control;
- allows children to feel safe because they learn to develop self-control from their parents' action;
- establishes a safe, positive and respectful family dynamic; and
- requires parents to choose their battles, and to control their emotions.

With a plan in place, parents' blood pressure will go down, and anger and frustration are manageable. Parents develop patience because they have a plan and have learned to wait for children to practice making their own decisions, which prepares them for independence.

The practice of minimizing words and maximizing action applies to tots-to-teens. You will create a more harmonious family atmosphere by issuing firm and friendly boundaries and following through without anger.

It demonstrates personal power to your children. They understand you mean business and you are in charge. They may *try* to be in charge, but deep down, they know they are not capable. It is overwhelming for a child to have too much power, and eviscerating for children to have too little power.

Write down your most pressing problem

In the spirit of starting small, write down your most pressing problem with your children right now; just about every parent has one, regardless of their child's age.

Here are some typical pressing problems:

"My three-year-old won't go to bed. He stays up, runs around the house and drives us crazy."

"My 10-year-old won't get ready for school on time in the morning. I end up driving her to school and I want her to be ready on time to take the bus."

"My teenager dresses in all-black. I worry that he's into drugs."

"My children are hard-wired to electronics and I can't get them unplugged."

Write down your most pressing problem now and tuck it on a piece of notepaper inside the front cover while you start implementing a positive parenting plan.

The broken vending machine

Imagine you put a dollar into a vending machine for a bottle of water and nothing comes out. The machine keeps the dollar and doesn't dispense a bottle of water. What is your response? Most likely, you shake the machine, hit it, tip it and flip the cancel button – and still no bottle of water or dollar.

Depending on your personality, you scale-up the assault on the machine and shake, hit and tip it, get angry, yell, curse and find the machine's owner. **Your behavior deteriorates when you don't get what you expect.**

The same thing may happen when implementing strategies from this book. Your children's behavior may get worse before it gets better. They may treat you in the same way you treated the broken vending machine.

When you don't respond the way they're used to, they will shake, holler and protest. They will refuse to believe the machine won't dispense water or refund their dollar.

Younger children will respond faster

This book is intended for parents of children from age 2 to 22.

If your children are between ages 2-11, adopting these strategies will lay the foundation for tolerable, even enjoyable teenagers.

If your children are 12 and older, there's hope, it will take longer.

Start small

Parents must be resolute: choose your battles, and start with baby steps. Don't waiver because youngsters can instantly sense a lack of parental confidence. Parents are a child's first and most significant teacher by what we say, and more importantly, by what we do.

No matter the age of your children, you can start today to respond differently to them. They might be surprised and attempt to convince you to go back to "normal." However, don't go back; don't be the broken vending machine.

Even if you are deeply discouraged and alienated from your children, find the optimistic part of yourself and try again. Pretend your children are stage actors. Create an emotional distance from them. Realize that in every moment, you and they choose how to behave. They may exaggerate their emotions to elicit a response from you.

Anticipate that their behavior may get worse before it gets better. This book provides a positive parenting plan. Learn the strategies and follow them, even when your children complain and tempt you to fall back into old patterns.

From caterpillar to butterfly

Some parents in my workshops protest when I suggest a different approach, saying "That's not me. I feel fake."

You may feel phony at first. That's expected. New habits take time to practice and internalize. View it as a long term experiment to create new habits, and have patience. **Mark Twain said, "It's easy to quit smoking. I've done it 100 times."**

Quitting smoking, going on a diet and learning new parenting skills require a commitment to develop new responses to whatever triggers you to smoke, overeat, or revert to old ways of dealing with your children.

To succeed at new parenting practices, make a commitment to become more conscious to replace old habits with new behaviors.

Start with small achievable goals. Think back to when you started a new job. You allowed yourself to be a beginner for three to six months and to get acclimated to new routines.

The same can be said for adopting a new parenting approach, with ambitious goals: to create a democratic family environment and develop teenagers who will make good independent decisions.

What kind of parent are you?

Parents typically either set too many limits, or too few. The trend in the new millennium is towards over-protection and befriending children. Strive to set fair limits and share power in a democratic home.

Here are four types of parents.

Democratic – parents and children have rights and responsibilities, with the parents as the leaders. Parents encourage age-appropriate independence and foster responsibility through family meetings, chores, the use of natural and logical consequences, and encouragement. This approach can develop resilient and responsible youths with healthy self-esteem.

Permissive – parents grant children rights and freedom without responsibility, possibly by sacrificing parental rights. Parents have difficulty saying "no" to children, which can create entitlement and self-excess-teem (exaggerated self-confidence). These children may be: given too much power in the family; left on their own to navigate; or spend the majority of time being cared for by others. Parents may feel guilty and indulge their children.

Overprotective – also known as helicopter parenting. Parents attempt to shield children from life by constantly intruding in the children's domain. Overprotective parents may show pity; give tacit permission for the child's lack of self-control; hold the child to lesser standards and hesitate to set limits. Some parents of children with special needs may use a diagnosis to justify over-involvement. Overprotection can create entitlement, set up a lifelong expectation of special treatment, and infantilize the youth.

Authoritarian – parents rule by domination, "father knows best" and corporal punishment. Typically, fathers have all of the rights and responsibilities. The children and mother must obey, without question or input, or face physical punishment, intimidation and/or verbal abuse. This approach can develop bullies and rebellious children and teens.

Avoid trying – do it

It's easy to *try* something new. Imagine that I'm in front of you now, trying to pick up this book. "It's just so heavy, I can't get my hand around it, it's just impossible."

When implementing a new strategy, don't *try* it. Instead, embrace it 100 percent, do it, and stick to it.

Imagine the whole family is in a stage drama and your new behavior is dress rehearsal for the new role of a positive parent. Learn the lines and recite them with 100 percent conviction. Eventually, the lines will come naturally and create new results.

> **Do or not.**
>
> **There is no try.**
>
> Jedi Master Yoda
> *Star Wars*

Give the new approach time to sink in. Positive family relations require practice, feedback, trying again and time. For me, it required reading, taking an 8-week class in a circle on old folding chairs in a church basement and talking about how to be different, and waking up to how my actions influenced my children's behavior.

You can't control your children's behavior. You can only control your response to them. You will learn new behavior in this book.

New practices: Have the courage to be imperfect. Everyone makes mistakes. View your family members and yourself as actors.

Challenge: Write down your most pressing problem with your child or teen on a sticky note on the inside cover. Set it aside for now.

For group discussion or journaling: What do I hope to gain by creating a positive parenting plan? How is my family of origin different from the family I have now? How did my parents influence the type of parent I am?

Key points from A Positive Parenting Plan

- The root of discipline is *disciple*. A disciple is a student. Our children are our students. We are the teachers.
- When implementing new strategies, anticipate children may react the same way you would react to a broken vending machine -- protest, shake and scream. Don't waiver.
- Avoid *trying*. **Do it or not.**
- Practice the courage to be imperfect.
- Four types of parenting styles are democratic permissive, over-protective and authoritarian.
- Start small, encourage yourself and build on success.
- Begin taking action and avoid excessive words and warnings.
- Read ahead to Chapter 17, *Name It and Tame It* if you're the serious student. It will provide much insight.

Even Hercules mows the lawn and does dishes

Kevin Sorbo links his success to the work ethic cultivated while growing up in Mound, Minn. Born in 1962 the fourth of five children, he learned early on about teamwork in the family's modest home.

"One brother would be washing the dishes, another would dry the dishes, another put them away in an assembly line formula," Sorbo said. Other chores included vacuuming, shoveling snow ("It's long winter in Minnesota," he said) and mowing the lawn. "Yard work is something I enjoy doing anyway. It's kind of a Zen moment," Sorbo said.

He appreciates the benefits of home jobs. "Family chores are a wonderful way to prepare for what's going to happen out in the real world. You learn how to be part of a cohesive team. If you learn how to get along with your brothers and sisters, you can learn to get along with anybody," he said.

Sorbo had a paper route. "From 8 years old until about age 16, I got up at 4:30 a.m. and delivered seventy-five papers on a bike in 20-degrees below in the winter. I put my money away and learned responsibility very early. I bought my own car with the money – a 1967 powder blue Mustang."

That work ethic has stayed with him. As an actor who constantly sells himself for the next role, he said, "I can't give up when things don't go my way. You've got to use every time you get rejected as a learning experience, otherwise you go crazy."

A junior high school biology teacher, his father used encouragement to motivate his family. "My father held the family together with soft thunder," Sorbo said. The children received a monthly allowance of 50 cents.

His parents expected the children to volunteer to regularly, without being asked to help, to do things like carry in groceries from the car.

Sorbo is instilling the same work ethic with his children, 7, 4, and 3 years old. "It's very important these guys learn responsibility," he said. The children put their dishes in the sink after a meal, take out the trash, help set the table, clean up their rooms and pick up their toys.

Sorbo has created a family environment in which his children want to pitch in without being reminded.

"I came home one afternoon and found my 7 year old son raking leaves by himself. He said, 'Dad, I'm just helping out without being asked.'"

Kevin Sorbo rose to stardom in the hit TV series, "Hercules the Legendary Journeys," and has been cast in a score of TV and movie roles since then.

Parents began to stop nagging and realized that they did not need to be slaves to their children in order to be good parents.
Rudolf Dreikurs

2
The Benefits of Chores Last a Lifetime

ummer Ice Princess

Summer Ice Princess

When I was 10 years old, my father took me aside in his basement sanctuary filled with tools to mold wood and metal, where he spent much of his free time.

"Susan, this summer, I want you to make ice for everyone."

"But Dad, the new fridge has an automatic ice maker."

"It won't make enough ice for everyone," he said quietly.

With seven people living there for the summer, Dad knew the ice bin would inevitably be empty when he wanted a few cubes for his iced tea.

"Here are the ice cube trays." He showed me four metal ice trays covered in dust and cobwebs. They were gross, ancient and awkward compared to the majestic automatic icemaker upstairs that effortlessly dispensed ice without spilling a drop of water.

Every, 20 minutes the marvelous machine announced the arrival of three cubes by expelling them with a clatter in the tall bin. However, the machine worked like chickens. It laid cubes only under optimum conditions. Even then, nine cubes an hour couldn't keep up with demand.

"If you make ice once or twice a day with these trays, it will give us enough ice for the summer," Dad said. I hated the trays and loved my father and wanted his approval.

Dad was a man of few words. He liked to work alone at home and as a research scientist at the DuPont Company. Dad didn't ask much or say much while he showed quiet dedication to our family. His main goals were to get us to keep down the noise, shut off the lights and use less hot water.

The ice project was the first job he ever assigned to me. I felt special. I accepted responsibility to provide surplus ice all summer for the family.

Doing jobs at home transmits values

The ice project emanated from my father's values: saving money by doing-it-yourself, using the equipment you owned (no matter how old) and planning ahead.

Born in 1919, Dad came-of-age in the Great Depression. Combined with the thriftiness necessary with having nine children, making ice fit in with one of Dad's fundamental life purposes: to save money.

It never occurred to me to say, "How much are you going to pay me for this?" Or, "Why aren't you asking Mary or Brian to make ice?" As the eighth of nine children, making ice offered me a way to contribute to the family that no one else could claim.

"Use these bags." Dad showed me a box of new plastic bags.

"Cool," I thought. The family rule was to use old bread bags with stale crumbs in the bottom. *My job was special because I was allowed to use new plastic bags.* It doesn't take much to please children.

I took my duty seriously and harvested about four pounds of ice first thing in the morning and again after dinner. Dad was right. The mechanical icemaker was inadequate. When we opened the freezer too often during hot weather, the temperature rose and it wouldn't lay ice.

Other malfunctions stopped production: cubes clogged the mechanism, the waterline crimped, and the ice tasted funny. On a good night when no one opened the freezer, it laid a small pile in the bottom of the bin, which got us to noon and lacked the sweet taste of my ice.

I felt proud when my ice was served with dinner and at Dad's weekly backyard volleyball game with other DuPont lab rats. When the ice bin was empty, I'd bound down to the basement freezer for a bag of "free" ice. While my contribution was rarely acknowledged by my father or others, I saw everyone using my ice during a hot and muggy Delaware summer day. I particularly liked to make ice when Dad was in the basement tinkering.

Chores teach lifelong habits

Being summer ice princess taught me a work ethic I still rely on today.

1. **Making ice at home saves money.** My parents avoided buying anything that could be made at home. For example, buying a $2.50 cup of coffee 20 times a month adds up to a $600 annual expense, so we brew coffee at home.

2. **Plan to make ice *before* we needed it.** My family complained if we ran out of ice. I learned to plan, manage time and inventory so we rarely ran out. The project management skills I gained made deadlines easy to meet in every job I've had.

3. **Delegate.** An effective project manager finds dependable workers. Notice my father asked *me* to be ice princess, not one of my scurrilous siblings. When in management positions, I can spot good workers by their work habits and attitude.

4. **Invest in good equipment.** I hated those metal ice trays and longed for plastic trays. To this day, I love good kitchen tools.

5. **Children want responsibility.** Children, especially under age 11, strive to please their parents, take pride in contributing to the family, and develop self-esteem from managing a task. Children will rise – or fall – to parental expectations. I was trusted to manage the ice supply and given space to experience the consequence of running out of ice. I hated to let everyone down.

6. **Take pride in contributing to the common good.** I felt good about myself because my family enjoyed the ice. It motivated me to keep making ice and view the job positively. The same can be said of tasks I perform today for family and friends.

7. **You don't always have to be recognized or paid.** Being of service to others in the world without expecting anything in return is a guaranteed way to make friends. Following that edict has brought me some of my greatest joys in life. Thanks, Dad.

When children have regular responsibilities around the house, the benefits reverberate for a lifetime. They don't have to be big responsibilities, take a lot of time or be done frequently. They must be **their** responsibilities, that don't get done unless they do them.

When children do jobs for the common good, they can experience being part of a community. Even though children may *say* and *act* as if they don't want to contribute to the running of the household, everyone craves the feeling of feeling important, needed by and connected to others.

Chores correlate to lower alcohol use

In a survey on childhood chores I developed for this book, the 564 respondents agreed: **childhood chores taught them responsibility and a work ethic.** The people who took the survey were between 11 and 92 years old, with a median age of 35.

One correlation showed children with regular chores around the house from ages 2-12 had a lower incidence of alcohol use in high school. Some 62 percent of the people who did chores regularly abstained from regular alcohol use in high school. There's more good news. People who had childhood chores were 24 percent more likely to report they were good college students.

Integrating chores into a democratic family atmosphere with mutual respect lays the foundation for decent teenagers who will use good judgment. Doing simple chores from an early age builds self-discipline, counteracts entitlement and develops teenagers who can handle freedom with responsibility.

Entitled children and teens are often protected from experiencing the relationship between their decisions and a negative outcome because parents constantly bail them out, make excuses and tell them everyone else is wrong, not them.

Cleaning a toilet, sweeping a floor, weeding a flowerbed, are sure cures for entitlement. It changes how one views work, self and the world.

Respondents agreed: chores prepared them for life.

"I was glad to know how to take care of myself, and do it with a high degree of precision," said a 51-year-old woman of her regular chores that started when she was 6 years old and continued until she left home.

I expected to find that chores had gone out of style, but 87 percent reported they had regular childhood chores. Of the 13 percent across all ages who reported no chores, nearly half were less than 30 years old. We found nothing else in common with the no-chores group.

Young people who had chores between ages 13 and 21 were three to four times more likely to report high educational achievement.

In my confidential survey, tweens and teens who responded made the following confessions about chores:

"I help out, and it's expected I do so, but I'm hardly held to it."

"Honestly sometimes these (chore) assignments are not fulfilled."

"It somewhat teaches me to be self sufficient."

"I don't mind working around the house. But I would rather not."

"I know I need to do it and it's good for me, but still…"

I heard a longing in the young people's comments to be held responsible to do the chores, even if they don't feel like it. Deep down, they know helping out is good for them, even though their first impulse is

Chores build self-discipline

Doing chores while growing up helped me in two ways.

The first is simple: I knew how to do chores. I was surprised when I went to college how many classmates didn't know how to do laundry, or how to change a vacuum bag.

The second is more a function of my parents than a function of chores: I learned how to manage my time. I was often given a deadline on when chores had to be complete. After that deadline, I wasn't allowed to do anything fun like watching TV, playing games or reading books until my chores were complete.

I received an allowance unrelated to chores.

This idea of "work before pleasure" really took hold with me, and I still operate that way today. I can never quite relax unless my dishes are done, for example.

I've never been a procrastinator, and I think this correlates with my parents' enforcement of chores.

Nate Chenenko, contract manager
Rochester, New York

to avoid it. It's part of the Yin-Yang of adolescence.

Parenting is a long-term commitment, as you know. Very long.

Like teens, parents sometimes have mixed emotions. Parents don't always have the energy, time and patience we'd like to have. If we show up most of the time and do the right thing most of the time with a good intention, it's good enough. We don't have to be perfect.

A chore system will eventually payoff. A 49-year-old woman from the Boston area who responded to my survey credits chores with developing life skills. "I truly learned a lot as I did chores that I now use to make my life easier today. How to remove stains in our laundry, how to cook for large groups on a budget from scratch, how to have fun while pitching in, and the old adage, 'many hands make light work.'

"I look back and realize how much I learned as I was growing up, what I thought as hard were things that other friends never learned, how to iron a shirt, fold linens, set a proper table, all sorts of things I never thought I would use in life."

Set up chore systems

Children with attention deficit disorder can benefit from chores and responsibility because it prepares them to develop coping skills. For example, Jamal has ADHD so his mother never expects him to remember to feed his bird or clean the cage, chores she has taken on. "I always have to remember his diagnosis," mom said, quoting Jamal's pediatrician.

Remembering the diagnosis is different than setting low expectations. Jamal's mother is doing him no favors by being his servant. Jamal has no

---

I help, Mama, I help!

Diego, 11, watched his mother and uncle fix the molding around a doorway in their home. He kept asking, "I help? I help?"

The adults kept sending away Diego, who has Cerebral Palsy. He can walk but has some motor control challenges.

Diego surreptitiously got a hammer in the midst of the hubbub. After the job was done and everyone was resting on the couch, Diego started pounding on the door frame calling out, "I help, Mama! I help!" The dents on the new frame were a reminder of the importance of being part of to the family's effort.

problem managing his time to play endless hours of video games and ignore his bird. Jamal and his mom need to figure out a system to remind him to care for his pet, or give the bird away.

Children with chores feel they belonging to a group, that the group depends on them. Show me a child with a job around the house and I'll show you someone with greater odds to become a responsible teenager, and an independent adult able manage his or her life.

Chores: The entitlement buster

Many children of the Millennial generation have been raised with a sense of entitlement. Millennials are also called Gen Y and the Baby Boom Echo. They were born after 1980 and have grown up with the Internet.

Some Millennials are surrounded by people who wait on and intervene to protect them from failure and conflict, including parents, day care providers, nannies, housekeepers, cleaners, teachers, gardeners, drivers, cooks, coaches, tutors and more.

Families caught up in activity-mania have scant time to work together at home or to value such time. Childhood chores and a family-centered life have fallen to the wayside, replaced with a frenetic lifestyle centered on two careers, affluenza and competitive activity-mania.

Chores are a powerful tool to develop resilient and responsible young people from age 2 to 22. Chores provide children with built-in autonomy. When adolescents have to choose between healthy and dangerous behaviors, they rely on a strong sense of self that is established during the first dozen years.

Childhood chores install the rudder and self-discipline to say "no" to peers who propose dangerous behavior.

Most children will never ask for chores, so it's up to parents to institute a chore system, which has deep roots in our culture. Adding chores to your family routine is not intended to add stress to the over-stressed modern family. A chore routine is intended to reduce stress by sharing the workload and prioritizing what's important to a family.

Slowing down enough to sweep a floor, make a salad for dinner or mow the lawn is good for the heart and soul of self and family.

Beware if you view chores as just "one more thing" to insure your children have the best competitive advantages in life. Simple acts of labor related to our daily survival have meaning beyond the surface.

Millennials are growing up in an environment where they are removed from performing essential daily life tasks, and from the earth that provides food and our home. Slowing down and working as a family is a long-term investment in your family.

The lost tradition of childhood chores

As recently as a century ago, children were essential to the dominant family business of the era: farming. Most school calendars still reflect the obsolete need to free the youngsters to assist with food production in summer.

The exodus from the farm lifestyle has dramatically changed what we expect from them.

In only a century, children shifted from being an economic asset to an economic liability. They are no longer active contributors to the family well-being. They have morphed into being mini-consumers and performers. Parents and paid caregivers wait on them. Divorced parents vie for their attention and time.

People have fewer children in the new millennium, and ask less from them. Out of necessity, larger families and single parent families are more likely to have chore systems, according to my survey.

Families orchestrate weekends so children can perform in adult-controlled competitions of youth sports, dance, beauty contests, creativity competitions, scouting, 4-H, pets, music and more. Instead of a childhood full of play and exploration, with some chores, children are routed towards being mini-adults with the goal to make their parents proud.

Children have also gained rights, freedom, and an unprecedented voice within the family, with correspondingly few responsibilities. They consume more and produce less.

In the competition to have winning performers, "helicopter parents" hover over their children's every homework assignment, soccer practice, and music lesson. Helicopter parents advocate for their children with teachers and coaches to insure the child is insulated from failure, which theoretically damages self-esteem.

Ironically, trial and error is often the best teacher. We often learn more from hard-earned failure than from easy success.Many children and teens live up to their entitlement with little awareness or apology in today's world where everyone gets a trophy.

They have been raised with the mistaken beliefs they can do no wrong, that everything they do is wonderful, and their demands often run the family. Without the opportunity to learn from mistakes, children never develop resilience and the courage to try again, try harder, or try a different approach. They want everything with a click of a mouse or faster than sending a text message.

Instead of developing character through chores, children ask for – and get – another handout from mom and dad, and spend their days suspended in sugared-screen time, consuming sugar and high-fructose corn syrup in front of a variety of screens: TV, computer, video games,

---

Don't just dream. Set goals and create it

From the 1980s through my teenage years, my parents owned a bait and tackle store on Long Island. Selling fishing supplies, bait, poles and more, "The Shop" was my second home, from age 5 on. I had regular chores, such as folding up cardboard boxes for worms, putting swivels and fishing accessories into bags, making signs, counting out killies (fish bait), helping with inventory, and more.

This shaped my work ethic as a child in the following ways.

1. It clarified how responsibility was a part of everyone's life, young and old, and made me more accountable and responsible;
2. It encouraged a feeling of teamwork within my family;
3. It instilled positive associations between work and personal reward;
4. It instilled a deep belief in chasing your dreams because owning a fishing shop had been my dad's long-time dream; and
5. It showed me that women can defy gender stereotypes. My mom did dirty work beside my father and knew volumes about fishing.

I am 29, a native New Yorker, and am *still* helping my dad with his business by building him a new website in my spare time.

Victoria Witchey   Lindenhurst, New York
Freelance writer--www.combsbaitntackle.com

---

iPods, Blackberries, cell phones and more.

Both parents often scramble in an outside career to support their children's ceaseless want list. They feel guilty over the litany of what their children don't have, and compensate by giving into their children's demands.

Parents have only one brief shot at raising children before their childhood is sealed in the hard drive of memory. By age 11, their belief system is entrenched and they become more difficult to influence. The less time parents spend with their children, the more difficult it is to influence them. When we give more things and money and ask less from children, it adds up to entitlement. We've become their servants. They've become performers and consumers.

Count on me

There is an alternative. Children can be re-introduced to the age-old idea of contributing to the family welfare, without pay, on a regular basis. If you employ the tactics suggested in this book, it may cause children, tweens and teens to cry out in protest, "I am not *your* servant!"

Indeed, they are not *our* servant, and we are not their servant. We are a family, a team that can work together using simple practices of family meetings and dinners, encouragement, and natural and logical consequences to develop responsible children who will leave home, and be self-supporting through gainful employment.

Doing chores develops responsibility in children at school and eventually in the workplace. It teaches a multitude of skills and builds genuine self-esteem -- not the self-excess-teem children have drowned in during the past few decades. Children can be told "no," that what they did is not up to par and they need to try again. They need reasonable boundaries and guidance from parents, the family's benevolent team leaders.

Many people who contributed stories to this book grew up on farms where they were counted on to contribute to the family's welfare from as young as age 2. The experience of being a valued team member with responsibility left a lifelong impression on them. Many of them are successful entrepreneurs and company leaders.

Your children do not have rise at dawn to milk cows in a cold barn or spend the summer picking vegetables to feel like people depend on them.

A few simple jobs a week will establish a similar foundation, without the farm.

Consistency is the cure

Being a good parent is like training a dog. A dog owner must be slightly smarter than the dog, and deliver a simple and consistent message. Dogs read non-verbal cues and respond to expectations. You cannot change the dog's behavior. You can only motivate the dog to make different choices by changing your behavior and using positive reinforcement.

Without boundaries, dogs can be dangerous wild beasts that can destroy your home and attack humans. When treated harshly, dogs can also become mean. Dogs do not have the capacity, to lead the family as Alpha.

The same can be said of children. When treated harshly, children can become mean bullies and emotionally scarred. Children do not have the capacity to lead the pack. They need boundaries and a leash. Children can be trained using the same tactics as dogs: by using encouragement, clearly defining Alpha, and setting safe boundaries. Good behavior earns them a longer leash.

The big difference between dogs and children is that dogs never leave home, but we want young adults to leave home. By age 12, young people can hold their own leash and must be ready to make good independent decisions.

It's easier to do it myself

Some skeptical readers may be thinking, "This takes time and effort. It's easier to do everything myself than to get my child to help."

Perhaps you have teenagers and despair of getting them to do anything they don't want to do.

As I say to my husband, "You're right, honey." Getting children to contribute around the house requires an investment of expectation, time and effort. In the short term, it is easier for parents to be slaves or hire people to do the dirty work around the house.

If parents do everything for children or hire help, children have more time for activity-mania and sugared-screen-time. Parents can accept young people's refusal to contribute to the household. Parents can criticize and shake their heads over shoddy jobs done by teens to sabotage parents' efforts and convince them give up getting them to work around the house.

Parents who quit will avoid the battle and lose the war. Such parents will become their child's servant and cultivate entitlement, which leads to battles that last longer than a standoff over cleaning a toilet.

If parents do not set up a chore system, they miss an opportunity to teach children self-discipline -- the ability do something whether you feel like it or not.

Being counted upon to contribute regularly around the house benefits children on a number of levels. They belong. They are needed. They are important. What they do matters so much that their parents are willing to follow through.

Sales training at Hurtte's Texaco

My dad owned Hurtte's Texaco in Taylorville, Illinois. I started working there as a carwash boy at age 9. Two years later, I started driving customers' cars into the grease bay.

At age 14, I ran the station until closing time at 10 p.m. I sold tires, batteries and other high-dollar accessories to farmers and negotiated the purchases of supplies for the station.

There were five children in our family. Everybody had a list of chores. We did not receive an allowance because my parents did not believe in it.

Every Saturday morning, before anything else, and Wednesday night after dinner, we swept and mopped the kitchen floor. This was a prestige job, because it was the one my dad had when he was a kid.

Daily, we made our beds, swept our bedrooms, and washed or dried dishes every-other-day. I polished everyone else's shoes before church on Sunday. We took turns caring for the family pony planting flowers and picking up roadside trash. There seemed to be an endless list of stuff that needed to be done.

My younger brother and I both selected high-profile sales-oriented jobs as our professions. We both credit our youthful experience at Hurtte's Texaco as the reason for it.

Frank E. Hurtte   Davenport, Iowa
www.riverheightsconsulting.com

Even when children and teens resist and yell at the top of their lungs, "I am not your servant!" make sure that they finish whatever they're working on. Smile to yourself and think, "Nor am I *your* servant."

Work can't always be fun

Walter's two teens have never had regular chores around the house because when Walter was growing up, "I had to do clean toilets, mow the lawn and do dishes all of the time. It wasn't fun," he said.

Walter and his wife either do the home chores or hire help, except when the tweens volunteer for fun chores. "When we got a riding lawn mower, the kids both wanted to drive it because it was fun," Walter said. "We'll see how they turn out with this approach," Walter said.

Walter and his wife are software engineers. Walter comes home to a plethora of hobbies. He and his son are overweight. They are a typical American family in many ways.

It will be interesting to see how Walter's children navigate in a world where every task is not fun, and jobs require self-discipline.

Expectations yield results

We parents do so many things for our children. Dreikurs implores parents to *never* do anything for a child that she can do for herself.

Would you believe that first graders can make their own lunch, with parents' assistance? Children are more likely to eat lunches they prepare. It teaches them responsibility and self sufficiency. It frees parents from the role of servant.

My children's lunches stood out at school. "Mom, most kids get their lunches made for them," Ian said when he was 7 years old.

"Really, Ian. How can you tell?"

"I just can." I suspect the mother-made lunches were neater.

Would you believe that children as young as 11 or 12 can do their own laundry? I got fed up with finding clean clothes mixed in with dirty clothes to be washed. I taught them how to use the washer and dryer and liberated myself from being their laundry servant. Children as young as 6 years old can operate the machines. Toddlers and up can help out in many laundry tasks alongside of parents.

Would you believe that tweens and teens can paint the house, babysit and drive younger siblings places, go grocery shopping, clean house, do dishes daily, cook and do yard work?

Would you believe tots-to-teens can contribute to the common good without getting paid? Money never changed hands for my children's contributions other than the standard benefits of room, board and a wide variety of other services provided free of charge. They received allowances until age 12 to be spent at their discretion. The allowances were never tied to behavior, chores, school grades, or used as punishment or reward. They were expected to contribute to the family and share in the rewards.

Life lessons gained by growing up on a farm

My five siblings and I worked together on a family farm in the 1950s and 1960s. My first outside chores were to gather eggs and tend the garden. Inside, I helped set the table and do dishes, starting at 2 years old.

As I got older, I was in charge of gathering and burning the trash. My father started paying me for farm work when I was 10 -- cutting seed potatoes for 10 cents a basket. That year I started driving the tractor and spraying weeds for $1 an hour.

I believe that the best way to impart your values to children is to work together.

When I married, one of our goals was to re-create that environment for our four daughters, without having to feed and milk cattle twice a day in the freezing cold.

We discovered that we had to be very intentional to create opportunities for working together that come naturally on a farm. Our daughters worked in our vegetable garden, raised and sold pumpkins and helped us with our business.

Millie McNab   Pocatello, Idaho
www.christianvalueslegacy.com

Put chore theory into practice

You might be thinking, "Getting the children to do chores is one more thing on my 'to do' list. I have a hard enough time getting them to get ready for school on time in the morning, do their homework, brush their teeth and stay away from the computer. I'm not sure I can handle one more thing."

Keep reading. The way to encourage children to contribute is to use a velvet glove combined with holistic a positive parenting plan based on encouragement, family meetings, mutual respect, and natural and logical consequences.

New practice: Become aware of your unspoken expectations and non-verbal language towards your children.

Challenge: Make a list of everything you do around the house. Don't leave anything out. Ask them to make a similar list with a column of what they do for themselves and a column of what they do for the family. Schedule a family meeting with the goal of moving some of your list onto their lists. Invite them to figure out how they can do more for the family.

For discussion or journaling: How did your family of origin handle household chores? What did that develop in you? What are your objections and suspicions of the proposed positive parenting plan?

Key points from *The Benefits of Chores*

- Doing a few regular chores each week teaches children life-long habits and negates entitlement.
- Hold a family meeting so children may volunteer to pitch in around the house.
- Expect and you shall receive. Set up a structure for your children to contribute and expect that they will.
- If they don't do what they said they'd do, follow through in a firm and friendly manner.
- Practice developing personal authority by taking action and using fewer words.
- Children enjoy the rewards of being in a family, so expect them to participate in the work of being a family.
- Your children might be secretly yearning to contribute to the family so they feel like you depend upon them and they belong to the family.

Genuine happiness is not dependent upon the attention of others
but arises from within oneself as a result of self-sufficiency.
Rudolf Dreikurs

3
Can I help, Mommy?

The first chore my toddlers did was to push wet clothes into the dryer after I took them out of the washing machine.

I encouraged them: "Nice job," "Thanks," "Here are some more clothes."

Next, I invited them to join in sorting the mountain of tiny warm socks, and gave more encouragement: "Look at the pile you made." "You're a big help." They found a way to belong to the family and be close to me.

The first job they took responsibility for at about age three or four was to empty the wastebaskets in everyone's bedroom weekly.

In these simple acts, I affirmed, included, witnessed, accepted and loved them. It set up a positive dynamic and created an expectation they will contribute to our family, and feel good about it.

Including them in doing laundry took extra time and attention. I could have done it myself, faster and better, in a rush to "get it done." I would have missed an opportunity for them to learn to contribute to the common good.

The basics to establishing a family work environment are the following.

- Start now, no matter the age of your children.
- Appreciate and encourage them.
- The younger the child, the simpler the task, and the more the parent is involved.
- Use family meetings to get the children's buy-in. They are more likely to do chores of their choosing. See Chapter 6, *Family Meetings, a Voice and a Choice.*
- Make it fun, if possible. *If it's fun, it will get done.*
- Tweens and teens require finesse and flexibility when following through to make sure they do what they promised.
- Most of the chores must be for the common good. Make sure the child is doing more than clearing their own dish or picking up their own toys.

Take time for training

When we painted rooms in our house, the children were eager to help, young and unskilled.

First, they watched me paint.

Second, they did it with me. I capitalized on their desire to be with me when they were younger than 11. It was an investment. I involved them in sponge painting walls, and painting simple objects such as a radiator, shelf or shutters, with plenty of drop cloths.

> ## How to teach a child a new skill
> You do a task. They watch.
> They do it with you.
> You do it with them.
> They do it independently.

Third, I helped them to tackle paint jobs. When Casey was 11, her bedroom needed painting. I asked, "What color do you want to paint it? What day shall we start? What do you need from me?" I became Casey's assistant.

Fourth, when the boys were in high school, I said, "Please paint the dining room during spring vacation while I'm at work." They did. It wasn't a perfect job, I could have done it better, and it was good enough.

Here's another example for a younger child of how I took time for training to teach Kristen, 6, how to set the table:

1. Kristen watched me set the table.

2. Kristen helped me set the table. "You set the spoons and cups while I do the rest."
3. I helped Kristen set the table. "Kristen, time to set the table. What do you need me to do?" "Mom, would you get down the plates from the cupboard?"
4. Finally, Kristen set the table independently, usually with a reminder. When your child takes initiative, encourage her.

This "time for training" can be repeated for chores for any age child. Older children can teach their siblings new skills by using the same model.

If it's fun, it will get done

Do not underestimate the value of making the job enjoyable through teamwork, encouragement and appreciation, and just plain old fun, like

---

Dancing dust bunnies

Buy micro fiber socks or hand dust mitts. Spray lightly with water or water spiked with a tablespoon of vinegar (the best non-toxic antibacterial cleaning agent).

Crank up the stereo, put the socks on your children's feet and dance while dusting the floor. Use old T-shirts and towels the same way to dry the kitchen and bathroom floors after mopping.

Blow up a volcano in the toilet

Children will fight for a turn to clean the toilet with vinegar and baking soda.

Make a spray bottle of diluted vinegar (half water, half vinegar) and a sprinkle-can for baking soda. Drill holes in the lid of a plastic peanut butter jar or reuse another refillable container with holes in the top. Let them combine the two in the toilet.

Add a dash of both to the toilet and the fun starts.

Vinegar is low cost, environmentally friendly and eliminates 99 percent of bacteria. Baking soda makes things smell sweet and de-greases dishes and pots.

Mixed together, they're explosive – and fun.

---

dancing around in socks to clean the floors and combining vinegar and baking soda in the toilet.

A 12-year-old girl wrote in my survey, "I do it because I have to and some chores are fun."

One Saturday when our children were 6 to 13 years old, Bob and I were painting the hallways and steps of our Cape Cod style house. The job intruded in the heart of the house because it included the two main hallways and the staircase. It was like a broken computer: life was blocked until we finished painting and cleaned up.

I painted the base coat the day before when the children were at school. We planned to sponge paint the walls and had enough sponges for everyone, including some of the children's friends who were visiting and clad in our old T-shirts.

Many hands do make fast work. Within an hour we had a colorful interesting sponge pattern on the many walls. It was not perfect or to standards Bob and I could have achieved **if** we had spent all morning doing it while the children enjoyed sugared screen time. It looked remarkably good.

At the end, the children were disappointed. "Can we do more?" they said.

Children and teens consider it fun to demonstrate expertise parents don't have. Youngsters can often out-perform adults in some areas. My children's homemade cookies were always better than mine because they followed the recipe and added 100 percent of the sugar and butter.

I offered encouragement: "These cookies are delicious. Your cookies are always better than mine," and ate several. Watching homemade food disappear quickly is powerful encouragement.

Like many Millennials, my teens were techno-savvy. Where would we be without our children to operate the remote controls, describe the latest online-gadgets and repair our computers?

Witnessing, encouraging and appreciating their contributions are more valuable than money or praise.

Everyone helps at the Children's Farm School

The Children's Farm School in Lake Elmo, Minn., embraces chores and communal work. Preschoolers regularly tackle "big jobs" to maintain the farm and school building. Founded in 1974, the preschool is on a former dairy farm outside of St. Paul. The classroom is in the old farmhouse surrounded by fields, woodlands and ponds. The school's philosophy is that children will learn, behave and become better people when they have a purpose. The daily routines are set up to incorporate chores.

"Big jobs" which require more than one person to work together -- include watering lettuce; winding up or moving the hose; hoeing or chopping weeds in the garden and moving them to the compost pile by wheelbarrow; making zucchini cake – sitting together to grate the zucchini and deciding together when there are two cups full; refilling the sand table, watering plants; assembling new furniture and more.

Teachers plan big jobs and are alert for spontaneous big jobs. They supervise, train, provide child-sized tools and create a cooperative and positive environment.

The children need no coercion to contribute. Instead, they rely on the Tom Sawyer factor. Children want to pitch in and celebrate the outcome.

For example, teachers start a day by providing shovels and spades for every child to help dig a diversion ditch to eliminate a huge puddle in the parking lot created from overnight rain.

Teachers asked the children, "Do you think the water is flowing in this direction?" "The children encouraged each other: 'Deeper here,' 'Dig over there.' No one wanted to stop until the problem was solved. The children cheered when the water began to flow out of the puddle." (Source: Nancy P. Jones.)

The school facilitates a self-sufficiency that is unfamiliar to children who have been bred to be passive consumers while parents, teachers, day care providers and nannies scurry to eliminate challenges and avoid mistakes. **Farm school pupils fulfill one of Adler's basic human needs: to belong, be needed and be useful.**

Teachers and observers notice that children behave differently after they collaborate to solve problems on real-life tasks to maintain their school and farm.

"Children who work together to drag a hay bale to the pony can better share toys in the sandbox. Hesitant children who are asked to help shovel snow become more confident when they later tackle new puzzles. Aggressive children who need to feel important become more friendly after helping pull cornstalks to feed to the pigs" (Nancy P. Jones.)

The Children's Farm School shows that twenty-first century homes and schools can create opportunities for children to contribute by meaningful work without pay or praise, when adults foster a different attitude and encourage participation.

Adjust your expectations

Adults can often do a task better and faster than children. Resist the temptation to re-do their efforts. If you must re-do, do it covertly so as not to devalue their contributions. Lower your expectations and keep in mind the long-term goal. Have patience and accept and encourage their contributions.

When expecting guests, I secretly touched-up the powder room. Bob volunteered to mow the lawn every third or fourth time because he wanted to cut the edges more carefully than the children did when they mowed it.

During the time for training, I inspected their work and showed them how to do it correctly. Later on, I occasionally inspected their work to keep up the standards.

Never too early to start

My mother was one of the top Avon ladies in the Pioneer Valley of Massachusetts, an endeavor she started in 1980 when I was 2 years old.

From my stroller, I was responsible to hand-deliver Avon books and orders to customers and to behave while my mother worked.

I grew up with the unquestionable knowledge that helping mom with her business was a family responsibility. In addition to selling Avon, my mom started working for two other direct marketing companies. At age 11, I took on a paper route.

My younger brother and mother followed suit. We managed three paper routes, my mother's three businesses and the household. I'm proud to say that I split the cost of my college education with my parents.

Today, I run my own business, and my brother is director of the loss-prevention division for a high-end clothing chain.

Trisha J. Wooldridge   Auburn, Massachusetts
Writer and editor--www.anovelfriend.com

"The corners of the meatloaf pan are greasy. Can you please come back to the kitchen and do it properly?""Who was on the dishes last night? Someone left a pot soaking. Please wash it now."

"The toilet smells. Whose job was it to clean it? Please come back and spray the outside of the toilet and the floor around it."

They grumbled on the call-backs, so I limited them. I enforced higher standards when I had time and energy.

Hire help or not?

Having outside help is a luxury. We hired a housecleaner when I went back to full-time employment and attended graduate school while the children were in middle and high school. The teens still had chores such as doing dishes daily and mowing the lawn, along with special projects such as painting a room. They supervised the youngest and drove her places.

After I finished graduate school and only two teens were home during the school year, Bob planned to escape the golden handcuff of corporate America. We made the family decision to stop the cleaning service and clean the house ourselves so we could save more money. Not only did the house get cleaner, $200 a month added up to $2,400 a year towards college tuition, plus taxes owed on the income.

Check your family budget. What are you spending on lawn care, cleaning and meals out that tweens and teens could be doing? Some employed parents delegate grocery shopping and cooking dinner to competent young people. It's an opportunity to encourage them to take on complex tasks, contribute to the family, and gain confidence and competence.

Children of dual-career parents can have regular responsibilities, but fewer in number and frequency. Keep them involved in chores of their choosing and hire as much help as you can afford or see fit.

The second shift

Housework and raising children are legitimate work that has been marginalized, ironically at the same time women have gained equal opportunity in the paid workforce.

Time and energy are required to create a home and care for children. Someone must be willing to plan and create the continuous stream of meals, routines, medical care and activities, to manage children and/or child care.

If both parents are employed, someone must oversee the cadre of people who replace the **domo-gurus**, my gender neutral term for stay-at-home parents who provide an estimated $134,000 of services annually if bought in the marketplace. Running a household and raising children require so much energy that full-time domestic-gurus can't do everything.

The women's movement gave women new opportunities and economic independence. Women inherited a double burden. We come home to the second shift, whether or not we have children.

Multiple studies show that employed women perform a disproportionate amount of housework compared to their husbands. Sadly, we women accept it and train our sons and daughters to fulfill the same prophesy. To change the expectation that women are house servants, expect boys and girls to contribute equally inside and outside of the house, without regard to gender.

Everyone at our house did yard work and took turns mowing the lawn. Our oldest daughter, Casey despised mowing the lawn and often paid her brothers when it was her turn. I didn't interfere because it was not my problem. The boys did dishes, cooked and cleaned.

Gender equity in housework starts at home.

Schedule the time

We scheduled family work time a few times a year when we had two outside careers and teenagers. It was often challenging to find an hour to rake leaves together. If everyone but Noah could join us on Saturday at 1 pm, we left a section for Noah to rake alone. It's more fun to do it together, but we all wanted Noah to do his fair share.

It sent the message to Noah, "We depend on you and value your contribution."

Tweens and teens have higher skill levels, and unfortunately, less motivation to use them. They become experts at inventing excuses, sleeping late and "forgetting."

If young people pitch in 80 to 90 percent of the time with a positive attitude, give them a "Get of Work Free Card" when they're tired, stressed or too busy. When Casey had a part in a play, she got a "Get out of Work Free Card" during performance week.

We always welcomed more hands on deck. When a friend gave us an above-ground pool, the children were between age 11 and 18. I asked everyone to help Bob and I set up the pool over a Memorial Day weekend.

Even though the pool was primarily my idea, everyone was willing to help because working together is part of our family culture. Noah's girlfriend at the time, Kendra, readily joined us in moving a ton of sand (yes, one ton) to line the bottom.

Like our own children, Kendra enjoyed the benefits of being part of our family and accompanied us on family vacations. Her presence triggered this formula: **Family plus or minus one changes the dynamic.** When another person joins a family temporarily, it triggers this formula:

$$X \text{ (Family)} + 1 / -1 = X^1$$

X^1 differs from X. The extra person changes how family members relate to each other, usually for the better. It was easy to add another potato to the pot and squeeze them into the van. Likewise, when one family member was absent, we all had one less relationship to manage and it shifted how we interacted.

Kendra spent a weekend with us at a condominium we rented for ski season. Every Sunday afternoon we cleaned together for an hour in order to return to a clean place the following weekend.

"Mrs. Tordella, is there anything I can do?" Kendra asked while I scrubbed the kitchen.

"Um, sure," wondering what was left to do so she could be a part of our family. The one vacuum was humming. One person can comfortably clean a bathroom. Others were loading the car. Wanting to include Kendra, I remembered a place that was usually overlooked and avoided.

"The entryway needs cleaning."

"Sure," Kendra said. Because the one mop was in use, I handed her a rag and a bucket of water to wipe the three-by-three foot tiled area. It was a five minute job to clean up several layers of grime, sand and salt.

Noah emerged from cleaning the bathroom and saw his girlfriend on her hands and knees at the dirtiest spot in the house.

"Mom, you asked Kendra to clean the floor with her bare hands? Gross! I can't believe you did that. She's a guest." Noah railed.

"Noah, she asked what she could do to help," I said.

"I can't believe you asked her to do such a disgusting job," Noah said.

Ironically, Kendra didn't mind. Growing up in a single-parent household, Kendra had more jobs at home than Noah. According to my survey, single-parent families are more likely to have a chore system in place out of necessity.

Kendra knew her contributions were valued and dirt is harmless. I respected Kendra for her willingness to pitch in. It made her a welcome addition to our family during the years she dated Noah.

The story has gone down in the annals of our family history as a test of new girlfriends and boyfriends. Another test is to determine if they're willing to make fools of themselves while playing group games like Charades. One boyfriend failed the Charades test, to our horror. He was soon replaced.

Children can be expected to enjoy the benefits as well as the responsibility of being in a family. When children have all of the rights and none of the responsibility, it's like a Petri dish to cultivate entitlement. You will become their servant. Parents need to set up a system, follow through and embrace the Zen of work.

When tots-to-teens have age-appropriate jobs around the house they receive an attitude and skill set that will benefit them for the rest of their lives. They will develop a discipline: to show up when promised, and do what was promised, even if they don't feel like it.

New practice: Schedule a family meeting and put up an open agenda on the fridge. Take a good time for training to teach children a skill.

Challenge: Have faith that your children will choose jobs they can handle. Support them to complete complex tasks you might think are beyond their capability

For discussion or journaling: How are you being different than normal with your children? What positive results are you observing?

A chore guide for every age
Toddlers, 18 months-2 years.
Every task is done with parents. Establish the expectation that their contribution is valued.

Push laundry into the dryer.

Match socks in the laundry basket.

Mop the floor with a parent, dry the floor wearing micro fiber socks.

Dust furniture with a damp rag.

Put toys away and pick up their room and the playroom.

Preschool, 3-5 year olds.
Able to perform some tasks independently, the remainder with parental prompting. Involve them whenever they show interest, such as cooking, hanging out laundry to dry, yard work and cleaning.

Empty wastebaskets in bedrooms and bathrooms.

Assist with simple pet care.

Put away silverware from the dishwasher. Set part of the table.

Recycle one category, such as paper.

Help with everything the family is doing

Give them real tools to use when possible.

Elementary school, 6-11 years old.
Parents do the chores with child until they can do them independently, with prompting. These are the peak years to embed a work ethic.

Empty the whole dishwasher, sweep the kitchen, and set the table.

Make their own lunches and snacks for school.

Take responsibility for homework.

Help do laundry.

Clean up the kitchen after dinner on a team, load the dishwasher, wipe the table, sweep the floor, take out the trash and wash dishes.

Clean a powder room and a part of a bathroom or kitchen.

Pet care.

Stack and move firewood, pick up kindling, shovel snow.

Vacuum and dust a room.

Rake leaves, water plants, wash windows, garden with others.

Perform simple sewing projects and mending.

Take responsibility for their room.

Assist with simple house painting projects.

Middle school, 12-13 years old.

Tweens gain capability. After a brief training, they are able to work independently. Tasks are more enjoyable when done as a family.

Do their laundry.

Clean the kitchen after dinner, including scrubbing pots and pans, cleaning stove and sweeping the floor.

Cook simple meals, take responsibility for an aspect of dinner.

Mow the lawn, shovel snow and rake leaves

Repair and maintain computers, bikes and skateboards with help.

Chop and stack wood, start fires in woodstove with supervision.

Babysit family members and neighbors. Pet care.

Clean a full bathroom.

Assist in painting a room, perform light household maintenance.

Work on a team to wash windows, clean a garage or basement, and clean out the fridge.

Do complex sewing and construction projects with assistance.

Work as apprentice for a family business -- for pay.

Keep their bedroom as they choose.

High School, 14-18 years old.

Build on their belief they have equal knowledge and ability with parents. Encourage them by getting out of their way and minimize criticism.

Independently perform any of the tasks above.

Teach younger siblings to learn any of the above tasks.

Clean a garage, car, kitchen, fridge, living room, or bedroom.

Go grocery shopping, prepare meals.

Drive siblings and pets places, run errands for parents.

Do complex construction and sewing projects independently.

Do yard work including lawn mowing and snow blowing.

Build fires in woodstove, split wood, and use chainsaw with training.

Learn house and car maintenance, such as how to fix a broken window and change the oil on a vehicle.

Be on the payroll for a family business.

College students and beyond, 18 years old and up.

Make adult-level contributions daily when home. Take on regular responsibility during long stays.

Leave their room clean before they leave for months. Cheerfully pull their weight and volunteer to help out.

*Encouragement is more important
than any other aspect of child raising.*
Rudolph Dreikurs

4
The Power of
En**courage**ment

I t's Monday morning and Jenn knows the school bus will arrive in ten minutes. Her daughter, Emma, 7, is dawdling, as usual, engrossed in a book. Her backpack is near the door, one shoe is visible and her lunch is half-made. Emma is dressed. Her hair needs brushing.

Jenn is getting ready for work and packing her lunch. She has been participating in a positive parenting group and learning about encouragement. At the last family meeting Jenn put "morning routine" on the agenda with the hope that Emma would take more responsibility to get ready in the morning.

Jenn noticed the clock and was about start on her usual tirade, "Emma, at the family meeting you promised to get yourself ready on time in the morning. You're nowhere near ready and the bus is about to come. What am I going to do with you?"

Instead, Jenn took a deep breath and said, "Emma, the bus will be here in ten minutes. I see you have the bread on the counter, ready for a sandwich. What are you going to put in it? Your backpack is ready to go. Great. Do you know where your other shoe is? What help do you need so you can get out the door on time?"

Jenn acknowledged what Emma had done and built on success.

As early as age 5 and 6, children can start taking more responsibility for their morning routines with encouragement, expectations and by setting up systems. First-graders can make their lunch, wake up to an alarm clock and be ready on time without nagging.

If you learn one technique from this book, I hope it is encouragement. It can transform your life and your family. It is a way of seeing progress, potential, and building self-confidence.

Encouragement is an approach to life and people that can be fomented from early childhood and used on family members, friends, yourself and work associates.

Encouragement is the fairy dust that can create a can-do attitude in your children and transform your family life, and work situation. It's difficult to talk about encouragement, and easier to understand it through examples.

Encouragement can have few words

One Saturday a year my father called for any of his nine children at home that day to help clean the garage. We spread the word and scurried across the street to the complex where he rented garage number eleven for $9 a month. We enjoyed working with Dad to create order among bicycles, sleds and big tools. We felt important and needed.

"First, move everything out of the garage," Dad said. Then we fought for one of the few available brooms to sweep it. There usually were never enough brooms, rakes or gloves to go around during family work time.

"Put the bicycles here," Dad said. We parked them carefully in a row, even though the spectacular new order would only last a few weeks. We felt a sense of accomplishment and like we belonged to a team.

A quiet man, Dad rarely acknowledged our efforts to clean the garage. It didn't diminish how we felt about it. We knew he valued our labor. Working with him was an important part of our family culture.

Praise	Encouragement
Evaluation by others I like it.	**Self-evaluation** Tell me about it. What do you think?
Addresses the doer I expected you to know better.	**Addresses the deed** That wasn't a good decision. What could you do differently next time?
General You are a good driver.	**Specific** When you allow enough distance from the car ahead, I feel safe.
Patronizing You are such a good girl/boy. I like the way Brittany is sitting the right way.	**Appreciation—Respectful** Thank you for helping. Who can show me the way to sit?
Conformity You did it right. I'm so proud of you.	**Empathy** How do you feel? I can see that you enjoyed that.
Judgmental "I" messages. I like the way you picked up your toys.	**Self-disclosing "I" messages** I appreciate your help. It makes it easier for me when everyone pitches in to help.
***Should* statements** You should chew with your mouth closed.	**Asks questions** Who can show me how to chew with their mouth closed?
Discouraging, focuses on final outcome You can do better. The blocks are a big mess.	**Courage to try again and keep going** *One* question is correct on the test. Half of the blocks are put away. Do you need help?
Sources: *Positive Discipline* by Jane Nelsen, *Honoring the Self* by Nathaniel Branden.	

The language of encouragement

Many people confuse encouragement with praise. They're as opposite as Antarctica and the Amazon.

Encouragement is a respectful way to acknowledge accomplishments, contributions, effort and participation.

Encouragement instills confidence and builds courage to try again after failure. Encouragement is low-key and focused on the deed, not the doer.

Practicing encouragement establishes a respectful family atmosphere.

Encouragement focuses on efforts made regardless of the outcome.

Encouragement is the most powerful method to influence the behavior of children, and everyone you know.

Courage is the root of encouragement. En**courage**ment gives courage to try again, even after trying and failing. Encouragement builds confidence to handle obstacles. Praise focuses on achievement, appearance and what others think.

To learn the language of encouragement, start by distinguishing it from praise.

Encouragement:

- is specific; praise is general;
- focuses on the task and behavior, not a parent's reaction to it;
- notices effort during the process, such as starting or taking steps towards a larger goal; praise rewards perfection and accomplishment only at the end;
- plants the seed to try again after failure; praise ignores effort and failure;
- requires that someone take a close look and appreciate the effort involved; praise requires little thought or involvement; and
- focuses on the doer and what the task, effort or achievement means to the doer; praise focuses on how the deed reflects on the authority figure.

An athlete in training

Mom says to 8-year-old Zoe, "I'm so proud of you. You won the swimming race" Saying, "I'm proud of you," makes the accomplishment reflect well on Mom.

Praise is typically high-energy and focused on success. No parent has ever said, "I'm proud of you for coming in last place in the race."

When parents take credit for a child's accomplishments, they must also accept blame for the failures.

Failure can be a powerful teacher. Learning to try again after failure is the only way we succeed. Failure is required for growth.

Encouragement gives children the courage to try again, often when they most need it.

Encouragement nurtures a can-do attitude.

Praise creates an inflated sense of self-esteem. What if Zoe came in last place in the swimming race? Would Mom say, "I'm so ashamed you came in last place?" An encouraging statement gives Zoe the courage to try again.

Destroying a barn opens doors

As the middle of three siblings, I cooked, cleaned and did laundry for my family while growing up on a hog farm in the 1970s and 1980s in rural Indiana.

On most Saturdays, I scraped hog manure from the graded cement floors of hog pens into a big pit below. When the pit filled up, Dad loaded the manure onto a "honey wagon" to fertilize the fields.

By age 11, I was babysitting, cleaning and mowing lawns. I got my first regular summer job at age 16. I tore down a barn that summer.

My parents never paid me to do anything. I don't think they could have afforded me. These experiences made me want to go to college and make a different life for myself. I'm an attorney.

A lawyer interviewed me to work at a law firm and asked about my work ethic and ability to complete projects. He hired me because I told him I tore down a barn when I was 16. I married the attorney who interviewed me.

We tell our 7-year-old daughter it's her job to go to school and learn and that we all need to pitch in around the house and work together to do chores.

Laurie A. Gray   Fort Wayne, Indiana
www.SocraticParenting.com

If Zoe won, Mom could say: "Nice race, Zoe. You really trained hard for it. Congratulations. Way to go. Your hard work paid off."

If Zoe lost, Mom could say any of the following. "Zoe, swimming is an individual sport. You win and lose on your own. It takes courage to enter an individual event. Your stroke looked strong. I could tell you've been practicing. Your time was two seconds faster than your best time in practice. That's an improvement."

Encouragement is low-key, and focuses on the child's feelings and effort – whether she succeeded or failed.

Praise focuses only on success. If the child doesn't reach the goal or perfection, they disappoint their parents, and get no attention for effort, which could have been substantial.

Encouragement acknowledges effort and plants a seed of courage to try again.

Find kernels of success

Sofia, 15, brought home an algebra quiz with an "F" on it. She threw it at her father and said, "I'll never be any good at math." Her father looked over the paper carefully and found one equation Sofia answered correctly.

"Look, Sofia. You answered this question right. Way to go. What worked on that one?" Dad gave encouragement when it was needed, after failure, when the teen is discouraged.

Anish, 11, showed his mother a watercolor painting. "Anish, you captured the colors of the sunset really well," is better than the generic praise, "What a beautiful picture." His mother had to stop and notice details about the picture to provide encouragement.

Encouragement focuses on how the child feels about what they have done. The child owns his achievement and the self-esteem from it.

Praise focuses on how the parent feels and conveys the idea that they own the child and the achievement.

Encouragement is a powerful way to generate self-esteem, according to Nathaniel Branden, a psychologist, author and self-esteem expert. In his book *Honoring the Self,* Branden describes twenty-four ways parents can nurture self-esteem and self-confidence in children. Many of the ways he recommends involve parent-child communication.

To promote a child's self-confidence, teach children:
- mistakes are a normal part of life;

- they have freedom to determine the course of their lives;
- their accomplishments are theirs, and not for their parents' aggrandizement;
- they deserve to be loved without being conditioned to perform to please parents; and
- to value themselves and their efforts, accept themselves, develop the courage to be imperfect and to try again through the use of encouragement.

Encouragement motivates workers

Offer encouragement when your children do chores and participate in life, with specific feedback, focused on what they are doing.

Encouragement is vital when children are learning new skills, especially when those skills are a stretch. Acknowledge the child's effort, whether it was perfect or incomplete. Encouragement communicates they can try again. A simple "thank you" is very encouraging.

The encouragement of getting published

My first article in print – about giving up playtime to care for my pet rabbits -- was published in the school newspaper.

During World War II, my father suggested we raise rabbits as a business and sell the meat, because rabbit meat didn't require ration stamps.

During the war, people had a limited supply of red ration stamps to buy meat at markets, so we had meat-hungry customers.

Dad and I built hutches for 160 rabbits in and around the garage at our home in Milan, Michigan. I cared for the rabbits. Dad killed and cleaned them. I delivered the meat.

I kept the money from the sale of meat and saved it, bought Christmas presents, donated some to church and more. I didn't receive an allowance and wasn't paid for doing household tasks.

Dad kept the money from selling scraped hides to Sears Roebuck, and paid for the rabbit food.

Lawrence O. Richards   Raleigh, North Carolina
Author of 200 books--http://demondope.com/site

Here are examples of encouraging statements:

"Katie (age 13), thank you for helping me to get the apartment ready for the party last night. Everything looked great. I really appreciated it."

"Billy (age 3), you put away two toy cars already, that's a start. Let's count each car that you put away."

"Tawanda (age 9), you vacuumed the middle of the living room. There's quite a bit of dog hair you missed around the edges. Would you please vacuum again?"

Praise or encouragement?

Read the following scenarios and determine which of the three responses qualifies as encouragement

1. **Allison, 17, bought the store brand of peanut butter when shopping for her family.** Her mother wanted natural peanut butter. Her mother says:

   a. "You could do better than that."

   b. "You constantly talk to your friends on your cell phone. Why didn't you call if you didn't know what kind of peanut butter to buy?"

   c. "I was counting on the natural peanut butter for a recipe. Next time how about if you take a list that has exactly what I want on it. Call me from the store if they don't have it."

2. **Manuel, 9, brings home a handwriting worksheet from school filled with poorly formed cursive letters.** The teacher marked it "F." His father reviews the paper and says:

   a. "I told you to practice your handwriting."

   b. "Look Manuel, here's one perfectly formed letter 'R.'"

   c. "Why does your teacher care about handwriting? Doesn't she know everyone uses computers today? I'll call her."

3. **Liza, 3, put away some toys she had been using in the playroom.** Her father says:

   a. "Thank you for putting those toys away. I can walk in here."

   b. "I'm so proud of you for putting away your toys."

   c. "You're a big girl for putting away your toys. Here's a piece of candy."

4. **Dwayne, 10, practices piano daily because it is his passion.**
   His mother says:
   a. "You're going to be a famous pianist."
   b. "I'm so proud of your piano playing. You're the best piano player in the family."
   c. "When you practice the piano every day, I can hear improvement."

5. **Robert, 4, brought home a finger painting from preschool.**
   His mother says:
   a. It's very colorful. You must have had fun doing it. I'll hang it up on the fridge."
   b. "That's the prettiest finger painting I've ever seen. What an artist you are!"
   c. "Mommy is so proud of you for making such a beautiful painting."

6. **Nikita, 15, starts taking responsibility to get herself up in the morning instead of her mother awakening her.** Her mother says:
   a. "It's about time you started to be an adult and get yourself out of bed in the morning."
   b. "You heard your alarm this morning and got up. You're forming a new habit."
   c. "I'm so proud of you for cooperating with me, dear. I knew you'd see it my way."

The encouraging answers were: 1 – c, 2 – b, 3 – a, 4 – c, 5 – a, 6 – b.

Parents often defend praiseful habits by saying, "I *am* proud of him. I want him to know it. What's wrong with that?" The problem with praise and pride is that children become circus performers for the parents' aggrandizement. The children don't own their achievements. Praise is reserved only for accomplishment. Encouragement can be given before, during and after an effort.

Encouragement is specific, low-key and focused on the task. Purge the statement, "I'm so proud of you" and replace it with the enjoyable art of encouragement. It will take more time, thought and involvement with the deed.

Wean the praise junkies

The dark side of praise is that it undermines the best parental intentions. Using praise creates a praise junkie who is externally motivated, focused on what others think, and conditioned to perform for the rewards of love and attention.

Children can lose themselves in the quest for praise and external reinforcement. They become puppets to make their parents look good. Praise can influence young adults to make school and career decisions on the basis of pleasing others and making their parents look good and feel proud.

Using encouragement requires a subtle shift in approach. The low-key emphasis is on the effort and the deed, not the doer. Praise is reserved for victory and accomplishment. **Encouragement can be used anytime, especially when a child most needs courage, to try again after failure.**

The forgiving nature of homemade food

"Susan, you're in charge of making desserts for the family," my mother said when I was 11 years old.

I started making desserts several times a week for the eight of us at home. I perused our family's favorite cookbook, Betty Crocker, renowned for its streamlined directions, use of readily available ingredients, and delicious results. I had the freedom to make whatever I wanted, and the responsibility to provide a sweet and appreciated finale for dinner.

I usually made double or triple recipes because my three older brothers ate like they were bears going into hibernation.

One afternoon while my mother was at work I tackled apple crisp, which called for "six apples, cored and pared." I didn't know the meaning of "pared," and lacked the patience to peel a dozen apples alone. It didn't seem important enough to call my mother.

I cut up the apples in eighths without peeling them, spread the topping over them and baked it.

At dinner, my brothers complained, "These apples have skins. Ha! Susan, can't you read a recipe? You're supposed to peel apples for a real apple crisp."

I watched them consume most of the apple crisp, in between complaints. Their comments were not encouraging, but their behavior was encouraging, because as usual, only scraps remained from the double-recipe.

The next morning I found a note left by my mother beside my bed: "Susan, I don't care what the boys said. The apple crisp was delicious."That tidbit of encouragement motivated me to keep cooking,

---

Canines respond to encouragement

Gonzo was a troubled soul when we got her. A black Labrador mix, she had spent the first two years of her life confined in a bathroom, tied up or on a leashed. Or so we guessed upon adopting her at 2 years old because she avoided bathrooms and ran away when off-leash.

Despite her harsh treatment, Gonzo is good natured. She just needed to learn to make better decisions.

We like to walk our dogs off-leash, and train them to come when called. Walking off leash was not in Gonzo's repertoire. "Come" meant "When I feel like it." "Stay" meant "No way."

Positive reinforcement and encouragement were the only way to train her. It was useless to punish her for coming back after she ran off. After all, she had done what we wanted and had come back, eventually. We ignored her when she eventually returned.

Initially, Gonzo's rate of coming when called was zero or 5 percent. She came by accident or if there was nothing interesting beckoning. The first thing we did was change the command from "Come" to "Get over here!"

She was not motivated to work for treats. Gonzo was a love-hound. She worked for affection. Every time she came when called, we over-reacted with happy voices and petting.

It took two years of patient, persistent encouragement to train Gonzo to come when called. Positive reinforcement transformed Gonzo's behavior. It took a long time, and it worked. We still encourage her with happy voices and petting when she does what we want.

---

even though my brothers rarely stifled their opinions on my efforts.

Despite the criticism, I gained confidence because they ate my desserts. I learned a motto I repeat to my own children: **it's hard to hurt homemade food.** Homemade food is usually ten times better than store-bought, especially desserts, even if the cook doesn't pare the apples.

My mother set up an encouraging atmosphere in her kitchen because we were allowed to experiment and mess up the kitchen. Those who didn't cook cleaned up the kitchen. She expected my three older sisters to cook dinner, no small task for up to eleven people. My mother's permission encouraged those of us interested in cooking to become accomplished chefs.

The power of pain

Much human behavior is motivated by the desire to avoid punishment and pain. For example, I prefer to get places as fast as possible, and I do not like the pain of speeding tickets, risking arrest and higher insurance premiums. To avoid the painful consequences of speeding, I follow speed limits.

I love sugar, chocolate and butter and would like to gorge myself on any combination of the three. However, I do not like the pain of obesity, so I modify my behavior to avoid the pain of being overweight.

I don't like paying federal taxes to pay for war. However, I do not want to be charged with tax fraud, so I pay my taxes.

I wish humans could be motivated without the threat of pain or suffering, but instincts tempt us to speed, eat sugar and avoid paying taxes. Avoiding pain and punishment and being praised are external motivators.

Encouragement provides internal motivation, self-confidence and the courage to try again after failure. Encouragement is more durable than the threat of pain and the reward of praise.

Practice the enjoyable art of encouragement

Practice encouragement by encouraging yourself. Say to yourself: "I am learning something new. It might feel phony or insincere in the beginning, so I will pretend I am an actor, playing a role."

Catch yourself using encouragement and give yourself credit.

Because encouragement is lower-energy than praise, you may initially feel you're letting your child down. You're not. You're nurturing genuine self-esteem, which requires years of fertilizing. Ideally, parents give children the space to develop their own sense of purpose, not dependent on parents' pride and desire for achievement to make them look good.

One way to test if a response is praise or encouragement is to ask, "Would I feel comfortable saying this statement to a friend or employee?" Imagine telling a friend, co-worker or employee, "I'm so proud of you." It's very condescending when said by a friend or an authority figure.

Catch yourself when you feel the urge to say, "I'm so proud of you." When you see positive behavior, effort or an achievement, practice the art of encouragement. Say something specific about what you've observed and ask the child how s/he feels.

"You remembered to bring your violin to school on your lesson day."

"You were ready to go to soccer without any reminders. Thanks."

"Thank you for making dinner. The combination of cheese with the macaroni is delicious."

Your children will begin to feel and behave differently. Your example will model the language of encouragement. Congratulate yourself when they encourage you.

Self-reliance relates to self-esteem

My parents enabled me to become a responsible person by giving me a taste of responsibility very early. When I was in fifth grade in 1980, my mother said, "Don't ask me to do anything you can do for yourself."

From then on, I usually made my own breakfast, school lunches, and learned to do laundry. I took out the trash with my father weekly and did yard work on Saturdays with them in Anaheim, Cal. My parents were still there for me, and I learned to be self-reliant and responsible.

It was very empowering and a big self-confidence booster to be able to handle responsibility, especially when I was young.

Living in New York for 15 years, and being able to take care of myself is paramount to success -- personally and professionally.

Richard Levine is an advertising copywriter
and actor, director, producer and writer in theatre/TV/film.

A group activity to learn encouragement

One of my favorite class activities to practice encouragement is to invite everyone to bring a homemade object to share, preferably something that is incomplete, has an obvious mistake or is downright ugly. Take turns giving encouragement to the creator of the object to give them courage to keep going and try again. Decide, together, if the statements qualify as encouragement or praise. This can be done online by posting pictures, documents and encouraging comments.

New practice: Start practicing the enjoyable art of encouragement. Catch yourself giving praise and revise it. Make encouragement an essential part of your positive parenting plan.

Challenge: Abstain from criticism for a week and replace it with encouragement or silence. Catch them being good and encourage them.

For discussion or journaling: Describe the impact on your children when you encourage them. How do you feel when you're offering encouragement versus when you're praising your child?

A comparison of praise and encouragement

Praise	Encouragement
I'm so proud of you.	You really worked hard to get that.
What a wonderful report card. I know your father will be very proud.	Nice report card. You must be happy. You studied hard and earned it.
These are the best cookies I've ever had. You are a great cook.	What did you put in these cookies? They have a delicious combination of flavors.
Your painting is so beautiful! What an artist you are!	I like the many colors in the sky. You put a lot of attention to detail into the painting.
What a big girl you are!	Look what you did.
You made the team. I'm so proud of you. The coach can spot a great player when she sees one.	Way to go. Your practice and hard work paid off. How do you feel?
That block tower is the biggest and best block tower I've ever seen! I'm so proud.	That's a tall block tower. How did you balance the blocks to build it so high?
You got the lead in the school play. You are so talented. I'm proud of you.	Way to go. That's exciting. How can I support you?

*I'll pay my children for what they do around the house
when they pay me for what I do for them.*
The author

5

Replace Pay and Praise

T ime to empty the dishwasher," I said to Noah, then 8 years old.
Noah surveyed the dishwasher. "Mom, will you pay me $3 to
empty the dishwasher?"

I looked up from the cutting board and considered Noah's
spontaneous test of my values. That's what I love about motherhood. I
never know what challenge will come next.

I thought quickly.

"Sure, Noah. I'll pay you three dollars to empty the dishwasher. Dinner
will cost you five dollars."

He was old enough to do the math. Noah emptied the dishwasher
without further question and I finished making dinner.

Parents just have to be slightly smarter than children. I'm willing to pay
children for chores as long as they can afford rates for my services, which
are many, varied and expensive. He might never sleep if he has to pay me
for everything.

Noah deserved a few points for trying a new strategy. Emptying the dishwasher was one of his several contributions every day. He received a weekly allowance, **not** contingent on completing chores. The children contributed to the family welfare *and* shared in the benefits, including an allowance for discretionary purchases and school lunches.

When the allowance was spent, no genie appeared to magically dispense money because Bob and I felt sorry, guilty or couldn't bear to see them denied something they lusted for or hadn't planned for. Establishing boundaries around money establishes mutual respect by conveying: "I believe you can manage your spending."

We followed the dictum of many financial advisors: **spend less than you earn and manage your affluenza.** We expected them to do the same.

If you pay children for what they do around the house and they don't pay you for anything, the system is out of balance. Children already receive free room and board, medical care, education, transportation, extra-curricular events, entertainment, and much more.

Children do not pay parents for services, why should parents pay children for contributing to the greater good?

Chores yield compound interest

From as early as I can remember, my brother and I had to dust, vacuum, clean the bathroom, help with the dishes, fold laundry, and mow the lawn. We never received payment for any of these actions.

While our friends received an allowance for taking out the trash, my mother said, "You are part of the household and you have to contribute to it."

I became a successful business owner while still in my 20s, thanks to the lesson my mother taught me: "You work because it needs to be done."

I'm now 32 and have a team of talented individuals working for me. I still focus on some less than glamorous tasks. They are important to make us the best company we can be.

Katie Gutierrez   Baltimore, Maryland
Founder and CEO--www.assistantmatch.com

When parents act as servants to children and pay children for their efforts at home or school, children have too much power and are at risk of entitlement. Parents will tire of being servants and go broke.

Money: a poor motivator, good manipulator

Paying children to do house work puts children in a power position to accept, decline or negotiate the pay. Money is a poor motivator because it manipulates people to behave the way you want them to.

Children learn to perform for money when they are paid for work around the house, earning high grades at school, or a specific behavior. When parents use money to control children's behavior, children learn to manipulate others with money.

Psychologist Madeline Levine sees many wealthy teens and their families in her practice in Marin County, Cal. Levine reports such youths are disconnected and depressed. In her book *The Price of Privilege*, Levine says teens find it more difficult to live up to parents' high expectations. Millennial tweens and teens suffer from higher rates of complex emotional problems, including depression, she reports.

One antidote to entitlement is to **quit treating children like show horses and start treating them like workhorses.** They don't have pull plows or wagons. Being responsible for a few simple tasks on a daily basis will suffice, such as doing the dinner dishes, keeping a bathroom clean or mowing the lawn weekly. Do not pay or praise them.

If you pay children for working around the house, you will win the battle and lose the war because of the poor relationship set up between work and money.

Money and work

Have you ever held a job just for the money? How satisfying was it? How long did you hold the job? Have you ever volunteered to make the world a better place? At work, do you perform certain tasks only because you're getting a pay check? Do you behave differently when the boss isn't looking? Have you ever helped friends and relatives as a favor? Do you feel valued when someone asks for you to help them?

The most rewarding motivation to work and serve others comes from within, whether money is involved or not. Working **only** for money is the least meaningful reason to work. It usually results in poor work performance and low job satisfaction.

If you're a manager or employee, think of the worst employees. They're likely the ones who are solely motivated by money. They slack off as soon as you're not around, watch the clock and have no sense of the Zen of work.

How to motivate without money

Remember the mantra: "I am not your servant." Unless you operate a family business or farm and directly profit from their labor, paying children to do anything at your house shows a lack of parental ingenuity and authority. Parents must figure out other tactics to get children to contribute, without using money as a manipulator.

Finesse, encouragement and natural and logical consequences can replace payment, bribery, punishment and reward, hitting, shaming, threats, overpowering and guilt.

My children had a choice: to do their jobs in the agreed upon time or meditate in their room until ready to work. They might have been denied the opportunity to leave the house. We abided by this rule: **first we work, and then we play.**

I committed to making "time for training." I picked good times to teach them that I meant business. When they demonstrated trustworthiness, they could choose when to do their jobs.

Most youngsters are not trustworthy. It's human nature to avoid work. Siblings can motivate each other by setting an example, criticizing or noticing jobs not completed.

Parents who want the benefits of children contributing at home must invest time and effort.

Getting young people to contribute around the house takes expectation, effort and a system. Children may respond angrily and resist when you make them do what they promised to do. That's part of being a parent. You are not their friend. Your job is to teach them a wide array of skills and attitudes, nurture self-esteem, and give them practice making decisions and living with the consequences.

Ideally, create an environment where they are expected to help out without being asked, like Kevin Sorbo's childhood experience. If that doesn't work, youths can learn there are repercussions when they choose not to do what they promised.

The leverage of expectation

In my survey, one-third of families paid children for doing chores. The other two-thirds either got nothing or an allowance whether they did the chores or not.

The younger children are, the less likely they are to receive allowances. Only 16 percent of Millennial teens report receiving an allowance unrelated to chores. The older generations got allowances at double that rate – 33 percent got a piece of the family wealth every week.

Giving allowances is not as popular today. More than half of Millennial teens said they don't receive an allowance. Only one-third of the older generations didn't receive allowances.

The section on the survey about money and chores generated more comments from all ages. Among respondents over 21 years old, family values and expectations were made clear.

Here's a sampling of the comments.

"It was all we knew, just a family duty. It was just expected. It was just the rule. It was just expected that we would. The whole family pitched in to help. Chores were expected to be done no matter how good or bad I was. We just helped because we were supposed to. Farm families all worked – it was just part of the family life. It was expected of me to contribute. It was what I did as part of family maintenance. It was a given. We were a family that worked together and helped when necessary."

Many simply said, "It was expected." Their responses communicated the non-negotiable reality of family work. **The one word that consistently described their experience was "expected."**

Expectations cannot be bought at K-Mart. They cannot be feigned or tried. Expectations are communicated through non-verbal language, by transmitting *this is what we are all doing now and it includes you. Get to work* It works. Young people respond.

Expectation plays a smaller role among Millennials, who barely mentioned expectation. A number of 17-year-old males who responded to my survey shared a pragmatic attitude toward chores and lack of remuneration. They left the following comments. "Because it's my house also. Because I live there. It is an expectation to contribute -- no monetary reward. My responsibility, they feed me after all. I get a bed to sleep on and food on the table."

Start with a family meeting

To win their cooperation, hold a family meeting and agree on a time frame for children to complete chores. Parents must be kind and firm when holding youngsters accountable. Humans naturally gravitate towards the easiest route. Expect children and teens may resist becoming producers rather than consumers.

Children might not be passionate about cleaning a toilet. Even though they resist, they may secretly find satisfaction performing an essential job for the family. Despite the smell of a dirty toilet, children inwardly cherish being depended upon. It can be fun when done on a team using the volcano power of vinegar and baking soda.

Externally, children may complain while we transmit the message: "Your contribution is valued. I depend on it. I love you so much I'm willing to make you do something you don't want to do."

Working around the house comes with the benefits of having everything provided for them. **With freedom comes responsibility, otherwise entitlement festers.** Children enjoy the benefit of using the family computer, going out to play or getting a ride to their friend's house, after jobs are completed.

Younger children will relish helping out and beg parents for a job. Once they own the job, their attitude may shift. Suddenly they forget and resist. This is when parents must commit to the value of childhood chores.

Teamwork makes it fun

Some of my happiest childhood memories are while doing the dinner dishes with my brothers and sisters while my parents read the evening newspaper in the living room. We fooled around, told stories, teased each other, motivated each other and occasionally hurt each other. My brothers would sometimes snap the shredded end of a wet washcloth and sting me. It didn't matter because it was part of the game of working together. I practiced snapping the rag until I could do snap them back.

My brother Danny is five years older than me. He liked to do the dishes with assembly-line efficiency to make more time to play in the backyard. At a family meeting, Danny suggested that the four of us at home work together on every night and replace two teams of two that alternated nights. We agreed to give the new system a try. A team of four with Danny at the helm cleaned up the kitchen in half the time it took two people.

Danny led by example by banging out the washing so fast that we could barely keep up. He made me want to be part of the team and work harder to achieve the group goal to play volleyball sooner.

You can create the same energetic by doing housework together. It becomes less onerous and more enjoyable. It is an opportunity for families and blended families to bond. Be secretly glad if children from blended families complain about the adults and the chores because they're bonding together over a common experience.

For a few years our family cleaned the house together for an hour on a couple of Saturdays a month. It generated a bustle of energy and teamwork and we enjoyed a clean house. For a few months, we treated them to breakfast, which didn't last because it took too much time. The biggest challenges were to get everyone together and keep them involved in the cleaning event.

When they were teens, it was harder to schedule a family work hour and we worked around it. We cooked and did dishes communally every night.

They were never paid for what they contributed to our family, even if I would have had to pay someone else to do the same job, such as babysitting, yard work or cleaning.

The only exception

Children who work on family farms and businesses deserve to be paid the going wage when their labor generates income. Many stories contributed to this book came from people who grew up on farms and worked in their parents' businesses.

None reported getting paid for "inside" chores, such as cooking, cleaning and other routine household tasks.

At a certain age, most began getting paid the going wage for farm work and in their parents' businesses. Those who didn't get paid for working in a parental business felt resentful. Many of the childhood workers who contributed stories reported they became judicious spenders and savers, and adult entrepreneurs.

Teach discipline and teamwork

Daily chores teach self-discipline. We relied on Noah to empty the dishwasher before dinner. If he didn't do his job, when it was time to do the dinner dishes, Casey would complain she had nowhere to put the dirty dishes after she scraped them. This removed me from the equation and got them working as a team.

If Noah was at soccer practice or sick, he might enjoy a day off from emptying the dishwasher. On a calm day, if I remembered Noah had soccer practice, I reminded him to empty the dishwasher before soccer practice, as long as we had enough time and it didn't develop into a power struggle.

In the twenty-five years my children were growing up, I emptied the dishwasher only a handful of times because I viewed it as *their* responsibility. The dishwasher was one of the greatest teachers because it was necessary, finite and simple.

The routine of children doing dishes together after dinner alone in the kitchen allows them to develop relationships and leadership. My children preferred that I wasn't in the vicinity of the kitchen while they were doing dishes so I wouldn't be bothered by the noise of their fun. At a family meeting they suggested I use a telephone in another room while they did dishes. I complied because it was a reasonable and respectful request.

Make your behavior worth imitating

Barry and Bev live together with Bev's two sons, ages 10 and 12. Barry's children are grown. The only task Bev, the voluntary home servant, requires from the three males she lives with is for the boys to clear their dishes after dinner and tidy up their rooms before the cleaning service comes. The boys have been diagnosed with Asperger's Syndrome, which is god reason to involve them in one household chore for the common good.

The problem is that Bev is the family servant.

"Bev will not let me clean up the kitchen. She insists on doing it herself. I have to insist on doing the dishes," Barry said.

This model is sexist, unsustainable and sets a poor example. The boys will not make good partners if they expect women to come home to the second shift and be their servants. Remember the example of Diego (page 26) who ached to help so he could belong. Bev's boys could benefit from "chore therapy," beyond clearing their own dish and cleaning their own rooms. My survey found that handicapped children were less likely to have had childhood chores. Handicapped children can be expected to contribute to the welfare of the household.

It's tempting not to demand much from the children in families where the children have a diagnosis, when both parents are employed, help can be hired and/or mom accepts the role of servant.

Dual career families need less stress, not more. Instituting chores can be as simple as taking responsibility for the dinner dishes every night.

First we work, and then we play

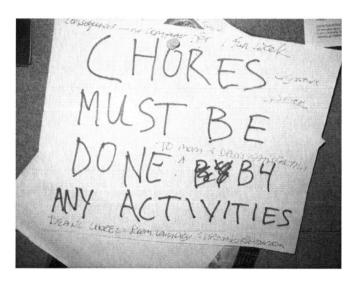

The small print in the photo reads, "Chores must be done to Mom & Dad's satisfaction. Consequences: no computer for one full week." Jacob has signed it. Jacob's chores are listed in small print at the bottom: "Room, laundry and upstairs bathroom." Jacob is responsible for a job that benefits the whole family: cleaning the upstairs bathroom.

The reminder is posted on the family bulletin board at the Anderson's home. Jacob, 16, was required to sign the agreement. Both parents are employed, with Mark as the domo-guru, an attorney with a home office. The couple shares the value that their three teenage sons will contribute to house cleanliness.

The consequences are clearly spelled out. Mom and Dad are prepared to follow through by withholding a pleasurable activity to Jacob -- using the computer -- until he completes his chores.

Doing chores before activities meets the test of being respectful, reasonable and related, defined as the "Three Rs" by Jane Nelsen in her book, *Positive Discipline*.

Jacob holds a part-time job at a nearby pharmacy. Chores developed a work ethic that Jacob brings to the job where he is a dependable employee. Computer use is a privilege and the consequences were set up in advance. It is reasonable. It is related because first we work, then we play.

Ideally, his parents chose a good time for training to show Jacob they will follow through and ignore Jacob's pleadings, protestations and arguments. Later in life, such skills may be useful. Remember, teens cannot be seen as too cooperative.

Ideally, children and teens will do what they said they would do in the agreed-upon time. In reality, there will be negotiations, half-done jobs, and forgotten chores.

As a result, they would miss the opportunity to develop self-esteem, learn the consequences of not doing their work, and not discover the Zen of work. Expect to be involved in getting them to do chores, expect to be creative and diligent about following through.

It is worth the effort.

Develop personal authority

As you know, the stakes get higher as the children get higher. My mother often said, "Children have youth, determination and stamina on their side. We're smarter, have all the money, and keys to the car."

Watching me in action with my brood, she advised me: "You have to develop authority, Susan."

To manage my children's behavior without bribery or punishment, I learned to act with confidence, authority and expectation that my children would do what I said, and what they promised by the time agreed upon. Mom's words echo in my head: "Susan, children can spot uncertainty in your voice a mile away. You have to be firm and take action *before* you get angry. You can't be lazy and be a good parent."

Many parents lack conviction, follow through and the energy to take action. They cave into their children's protests because they out of guilt, or because they don't take time for training or for nature to take its course. **When parents lack conviction in their authority, their children are often out of control.**

The only way to develop personal authority is to practice it. Expect them to push back. Expect them not to like it when you say "no." Expect them to test your resolve. Avoid guilt. Avoid the temptation to develop authority by being a bully and using corporal punishment. Say what you mean and mean what you say. Pick your battles. **Young people will respond with respect when you take a stand.**

For example, Margo is divorced with four children. When Bill moved in, they had a fifth child. Her 7-year old son Beau often said to Bill, "I hate you. I hope you go away," and called him names.

Margo got fed up. "I couldn't stand it anymore. I called a family meeting and said, 'Bill is a part of this family and he is here to stay. It is not acceptable to treat him that way," said Margo, who is receiving coaching on how to set more firm and consistent limits.

With a positive parenting plan, Margo gave Beau a choice: "If you are going to speak to Bill or anyone else that way, you can leave the room." Bill now responds with assurance: "No matter what you say, Beau, I am not going anywhere."

The new response diffuses the confrontation and gives Beau a choice without threats or punishment. Beau can stop the verbal abuse or leave the room.

In another example, best-selling author James Patterson reinforced his values with his 11-year-old son one summer. Instead of chores, he told his

---

Conquer a dirty bathroom with teamwork

Kristen's four college roommates use a team strategy to keep their one heavily-used bathroom clean.

Each person cleans one part: the tub, toilet, sink, mirror and linens, or floor.

Scrubbing their individual parts only takes only a few minutes and the bathroom stays relatively clean.

Families can use the same strategy and children as young as 5 or 6 years old can be in charge of cleaning one part of the room.

---

son he had to read one hour a day. The first summer the boy opposed the campaign. During the second summer, expecting him to read good books for one hour captured the boy's interest in reading, without payment as a reward.

Avoid servitude

In the rush to get things done and move onto the next activity, it would have been easier to do everything myself. Because my husband Bob avoided conflict and despised making someone do something they didn't want to, I sometimes had to prevent him from doing the children's jobs.

With four children, it was impossible to be their servant. It is easier for parents of one or two children to fall into the role of servants. However, with fewer children, it is also easier for parents to keep track of the children's jobs and to follow through.

Sometimes the children weaseled out of their chores. I've heard every conceivable excuse and witnessed scores of clever strategies to avoid completing chores. They would plead, "I have to do my homework," "Meghan is coming over," "I'll do it later," hide out in the bathroom, and feign illness.

If I pay someone else for the job

"If I'm going to pay someone else to do the job anyway, then I might as well pay my child to do it for me," said Joe, who paid his children to wash his car. "I was going to pay the carwash $12," he explained.

I disagree with that philosophy. First, it's better for the environment to have the soapy water treated in a storm water system at the carwash instead of washing down the driveway into the sewer system.

Second, it falls into that nebulous territory of parents manipulating children to do something for them in exchange for money. If children pay parents for doing special jobs like taking them out for ice cream or buying them new shoes, I agree, parents can pay children to wash the car.

If children want to earn money, they can get hired by someone else.

The same argument holds true for teens that care for younger siblings. "I would have to pay a babysitter, why shouldn't I pay Morgan to babysit?"

The answer is Morgan enjoys myriad benefits of living in your home and can make a contribution to the greater good.

I was grateful to my older children when we didn't have to hire babysitters anymore and they could stay home together peacefully when we went out. They enjoyed the freedom to stay up a little later and the treats of special foods and movies. I encouraged them by saying, "Thanks. I appreciate you being in charge when we go out."

When "Casey babysitting" came up on the family meeting agenda, we agreed to let them use paper plates for dinner and decided together how to manage TV and bedtime routines without us around. The notes read, "Everyone in their pajamas before starting the movie. Must go to bed when it's time."

New practice: If you have been paying children for chores, have a family meeting and announce you will begin paying weekly allowances only, with no extra payments if they run out. If they're older than 11, say, "I bet you could find ways to earn money." If they're less than 11, say, "I bet you can learn to plan how to spend your allowance."

Challenge: Use encouragement, teamwork, agreed-upon deadlines, kind and firm follow-through and appreciation to engage children in doing the chores they agree to. Start small with one or two chores.

For discussion or journaling: How did your family of origin handle money? What did that develop in you? What are your children's responses to the new practices and systems? What does it feel like to develop personal authority?

Ten strategies to create a team environment

1. Expectations are like fairy dust. Expect they will contribute to the maintenance of your home.
2. Model the Zen of work, that work can be fun and you enjoy working together. Show pride in your work.
3. If you have more than one child, let them work together without adult supervision.
4. Use family meetings to decide who will do chores what by what time, and the consequences if they don't. See the next chapter.
5. **Encourage them.** Encouragement, acknowledgement and appreciation are priceless ways to nurture self-esteem and witness your children's efforts.
6. Take time for training. Teach them how to do the job, and hold them to the agreements, with kindness and firmness. If needed, choose a good time to demonstrate you will hold them to their promises.
7. Manage your behavior. Develop parental authority. Say what you mean and mean what you say. Choose your battles.
8. Take action before you get angry. Anger is always a choice, even if it is chosen unconsciously, in a split second. If you can't change the situation, plan a different response to it.
9. Be flexible and accommodate their feelings and schedules unless they take advantage of it.
10. Keep an eye on the long-term vision, especially if you're just starting to implement chores with older children. Anticipate resistance. Respond with quiet determination. Even though teens say they don't want to help, they like to be needed and part of the group.

The family is the most fundamental unit of society.
14th Dalai Lama

6
Family Meetings:
A Voice and a Choice

amily meetings are a powerful technique to create a harmonious home and nurture young people to make good independent decisions. Family meetings incorporate mutual respect, natural and logical consequences, and are a way to defuse power struggles. Family meetings are an ideal venue for encouragement.

It's highly encouraging for a young person to run the meeting, and to have their ideas discussed and adopted. Give their proposals a trial run for a week, even if they're not perfect. It gives children the experience that it's okay to take risks, and try again.

Regular family meetings are a place to agree upon chores, settle disagreements, plan events and excursions, communicate, negotiate and have fun together. Children and parents take turns running the meetings and taking notes.

Family meetings establish a cooperative environment and a place to practice mutual respect, which is one of the tenets of self-esteem, according to Nathaniel Branden. When parents respect their children, it affirms the child's dignity, and proves parents take seriously the child's desires, ideas and needs. **A child treated with respect learns self-respect.** Children are empowered at family meetings when they are seen and heard by parents, and negotiate limits and privileges.

Family meetings also allow parents to resign from being their child's servant and get children to contribute to the family. At family meetings, children make a public commitment to do a chore, agree on the completion goal and the consequence if it is not done. Chores and family meetings provide a place for children to belong in the family.

The first family meeting

A child can create an agenda template similar to the example, print it on a standard sheet of paper and make blank copies for future meetings. Handwritten agendas work, too. Begin keeping an open family meeting agenda posted on the fridge between meetings so children and parents may write down issues as they arise, with their name. For example, "Drying the dishes – Mom," and "Bedtime – Dave."

It is essential that parents model using the agenda between meetings. Knowing a problem will be addressed

Family Meeting Agenda
Facilitator_____
Scribe_____
Date_____
Reading of the Minutes
Compliments
New Business   Name
_____
_____
_____
Plan family fun for the week. Have a special treat.

at a future meeting can diffuse tension in the moment and plant a seed of hope for the future.

Every family meeting provides an opportunity to bond, work together as a team, solve problems, develop leadership and negotiating skills, and have fun.

We held family meetings once or twice a month. Even if there is no new business, it is worthwhile to hold a family meeting to give compliments to each other, share a special food, and have family fun on the spot. New business might arise spontaneously.

The family meeting follows a routine with the roles of facilitator and scribe (note-taker). The meeting opens with an exchange of compliments, followed by new and old business – issues that people put on the agenda before and during the meeting. The meeting closes with a plan for family fun and a special treat to eat. Family fun can take place immediately after the meeting or later.

Facilitator

Children as young as 5 years old who have attended previous meetings can facilitate, with support from a parent. The younger they are, the more they will cherish being in charge of the meeting and the more endearing it is to watch them in action.

Scribe

Scribes need to be able to write quickly and legibly. By age 10, most children can write well enough to be the scribe. Bob and I often volunteered to take notes because the children weren't fond of taking notes and we wanted to make the meetings enjoyable.

While taking notes is hard, it is important everyone takes a turn at this least-desirable and crucial role, as soon as they are able. Each scribe takes a different slant on the discussions.

A decade later, I shared the family meeting notes I had saved, and we all laughed at the memories. **Notes taken by children were more interesting than notes taken by parents.**

Reading of the minutes

Take time to review decisions made at the previous meeting by having the previous scribe read the minutes from the last meeting. Include compliments – or not – as part of the minutes.

Favorite excerpts from family meeting notes

The following notes taken by my children are from various family meeting minutes when the children were between 5 and 17 years old. At the time of the first entry, we had just bought new kitchen chairs with rush seats.

New chair shredding. DO NOT MOUNT CHAIR. MOM IS ANGRY. Ian suggested Mom go to parenting class. (My own.)

Casey will read to Ian when babysitting, Noah will read to Kris. Use paper plates (for dinner).

Do not chase Boomer (the dog) around house.

Noah tapping. Noah only stops tapping if Mom and Dad are around. If Noah is asked nicely, please stop tapping. Use drum set.

Needle nose pliers/power tools. Dad has missing tools. Dad has to buy tools. Return Tools.

Turn off lights and heat ... ALWAYS. Shut them off! Electric bill$.

Dishwasher – Empty it now, darn it! Before 6 pm.

Ian's socks. They are everywhere. Ian -- pick them up. Dad is missing socks. People lose socks → stop stealing them.

Help fix dinner willingly.

Don't eat after 5 p.m. Only nutritional (sic) snacks.

When Mom is not present, kitchen does not get cleaned adequately.

Shampoo: Casey. Please do not use. Casey must leave (shampoo and conditioner bought with her own money) under sink. She will sell squirts 15 cents each or 30 cents for both.

Rescue 911: will no longer watch. Too violent. (Rescue 911 was a TV show in which 911 calls were re-enacted. It caused anxiety.)

Favorite meals: pizza, shrimp, box macaroni and cheese, Spanish omelets, mashed potatoes, rice pilaf, rice with chicken, chocolate chip cookies, barbeque.

Grandma visiting – Mom. Do what Grandma says. Do dishes. Do things for her. Don't complain. TAKE care of Boomer. Walk dog together.

Allowances Noah. 25¢ per year of life. Passed.

Compliments

Keep compliments simple. Record them so they can be heard at the meeting and then re-read them as part of the minutes of the next meeting. My children consistently voted down the practice of re-reading compliments and objected to writing them down. We finally agreed that the facilitator could determine the compliment format. I insisted they be recorded and volunteered to do so for the scribe.

Here are some formats to give each other compliments.

- Go around the table and offer compliments to anyone. Parents must ensure everyone receives at least one compliment.
- Give a single compliment to the person to the right or left of you.
- Give a general compliment on something you like about the family.
- Put everyone's name in a hat and draw. Give a compliment to that person.

Keep compliments light. The family pets can be included for fun. When we celebrated someone's birthday, everyone said what they like about that person at dinner. Practicing giving and receiving compliments builds a sense of self in the givers and receivers. It is a valuable practice for siblings and step-siblings to see the good in each other, even if they find it hard to get along.

Regular business: dogs, dishes and decisions

Dog care, dishes and sibling conflicts appeared regularly on our family meeting agendas. The succession of family dogs provided a topic we all cared passionately about and worked together to solve. I was adamant that the children participate in dog care because it was their dog, not mine.

The dog united us as a family in myriad ways. An excerpt from the family meeting notes taken by Noah, 9, reads: "What it means to have a dog" by Mom. "Must love it, walk it, feed it. You must be fair with it and pay for its food. Train it. Work as a team to care for and bathe it. Talk to it. Clean up after it. Brush it. IT IS WORTH IT. Who wanted a dog? Noah, Casey, Ian, Kristen, Dad, ~~Mom.~~ Mom gets very angry when people don't take care of it. Mom will keep track of gripes."

Most democratic family meetings:

- Are a forum to discuss and solve problems, volunteer for chores, and defuse conflict;
- Create an atmosphere of mutual respect;
- Nurture a child's self esteem by establishing a place to belong, be seen and heard and contribute;
- Provide a record of agreements made, as well as a source of memories;
- Are essential for blended families; and
- Are fun and productive.

Family meetings create cohesion

Susan's positive parenting workshop inspired me to conduct regular family meetings on Sunday evenings. At first, my four children participated grudgingly; however, soon it became a positive part of our weekends.

During the meetings we took turns keeping notes, discussing highs and lows of the previous week, what we were looking forward to and/or dreading in the upcoming week, offering suggestions for what to have for dinner, and more.

Discussing each child's highs and lows encouraged the kids to share their thoughts and feelings in a safe environment. They became mindful of their differences and earned each other's respect.

We created a chore list and rotated them weekly. One child was designated as the "child of the week." She or he was free from chores and could pick a favorite dessert to have for dinner.

Even the youngest child had a chore. The older kids became teachers to the younger ones and gave all of the kids a feeling of pride and satisfaction.

Some meetings lasted for an hour and we finished with a family activity such as a board game. Some meetings were frustrating because we were tired or grumpy, so the meeting lasted only a few minutes.

I learned to be mindful of each child as individuals, to respect their busy lives, and realized that my agenda may not be their agenda.

I looked forward to those Sunday evening meetings. We were six in a room together, respecting each other, and a united family. My children are now age 18 through 26. Perhaps, someday, when they become parents they will continue the tradition of family meetings. I certainly hope so.

Barbara Caldwell-Miller   Littleton, Massachusetts

The children knew too much complaining about dog care could trigger giving the dog away because the consequence met the requirements of the three Rs. It was related, reasonable and respectful.

Three dogs later, I recommend families, especially blended ones, have a dog because a dog unites a family like nothing else. Caring for, loving, making decisions for and telling stories about a dog brings everyone together in a common cause.

When one of my children was furious with me, I could miraculously change his or her mood by saying, "Do you know what Boomer did today?" I still save up funny dog stories about Gonzo to share.

At family meetings we decided on dog care and even what language to use when training the dog. We used the words "Remain stationary" instead of "Stay." "Hold it" meant, "Don't run out the door."

We trained dogs with the same consistency we trained children. Dog ownership came with a cost of time and money and brought benefits that far outweighed the cost. Dog ownership guaranteed something to talk and laugh about at family meetings and meals.

Doing dishes teaches negotiation skills

Dishes were an ongoing source of discussion at family meetings. Ian wrote on the agenda on the fridge, "Dishes – Ian." The notes read: "Problem: Ian feels when he does the dishes, he hates it." Noah, the scribe, didn't elaborate on the discussion. He summarized the solution: "The people will try to be nice."

Dad put "dishes" on the agenda. "One certain person needs to focus more" (on doing the dishes -- Ian). "Ideas? "Do them quickly. Just get working. Go as fast as possible." And "Mist Ian when loafing." At the time, we used a spray bottle of water to train Boomer by misting him.

Ironically, Ian grew up to be a super-dishwasher, and enthusiastically attacks a huge pile of dishes. He worked as a dishwasher at a delicatessen during high school and criticized the poor work ethic of other dish-washers.

At another meeting Noah proposed creating a Lego™ room in the dining room. The notes read: "Dad thinks we should eat in the DINING ROOM. Eat with candles and table cloths. Kids need dining room for LEGOS." We relented and allowed the children to leave Legos™ set up on the dining room table for months. It looked sloppy, yet the room was rarely used. Instead of banishing the children to the basement, they enjoyed a cheerful Lego room beside a bay window.

Other issues were non-negotiable, such as paying children for chores, getting a second dog, or skipping family dinner. They could put such issues on the family meeting agenda, and we vetoed them. They showed interest in the process and participated in it, including compromising.

Boomer the agenda hound

Boomer was an ongoing group project for our family who united, aggravated and amused us. Here are some highlights from the family meeting notebook about our first dog.

"Boomer learned how to shake!"

"Boomer water: one is out in the yard, one on the porch and one by the newspaper recycling. Period. "

"Boomer walks: boys will rotate in the morning, Casey after school. ≥10 minutes."

"Mom does not want to walk dog. Dad will do it Sunday. Kids will do it on Saturday. Put inishals (sic) on calendar."

"Boomer: teach him right and left paws, suggested Casey. No more begging. Keep on rope. Let out in dark OK no leash. Use 'snickies' not 'treats' when offering him a dog treat. By using the same vocabulary, Boomer would learn the words and commands better."

"Boomer's leftovers – Kristen (5 years old). Kris thinks Boomer should be allowed to eat leftovers. Children thought Boomer would gain weight. Food wouldn't be wasted if Boomer ate it. Boomer would get used to table food. Rejected."

"Boomer – Monday – Ian walk Boomer with Mom, Tuesday – Noah, Thursday – Kristen, Friday – Bob." (I eventually surrendered to pet ownership and walked Boomer with the children.)

Under compliments: "Kids like the way Mom is liking Boomer." (They wanted me to love the dog as much as them.)

When Boomer got hit by a car and died when he was 18 months old, I cried along with the children. Through their tears, they asked, "Can we get another dog?" Of course we did.

There are appropriate and inappropriate issues for family meetings. We kept the level of problems simple and related to their lives.

Family meetings were useful to prepare for grandparents' visits. When my mother Mildred arrived for a week to care for the children, ages 12, 10, 9 and 6, she attended the family meeting.

I put on the agenda: "Grandma's Stay – Mom." Casey's notes read: "Kids should do these things to make Grandma's stay easier: quiet dinners, finish everything (homework and jobs) before dinner, (watching) Jeopardy and pajamas. FUN: go to movies and to Wendy's."

My mother participated in the family meeting. We explained the Saturday morning cleaning regime. The notes read, "Grandma suggested we all stay in bed or rooms quietly (on Saturday and Sunday). Ian will be Grandma's alarm clock at 7:30 a.m." They followed the agreement and Grandma got some extra sleep on the weekend.

Family Fun

Family fun can be short and simple and held right after the meeting. It can be held later and be as complex as going on vacation together. Family fun can be an activity the whole family was going to do together anyway.

Examples of bigger events include going: to another family's house for a cookout; on a walk in the woods with the dog; canoeing; to visit grandparents; to an amusement park; skiing; and out for ice cream or dinner.

When we had several teens, family fun was more challenging to schedule and agree upon. We were not big TV watchers, but for a few years, we watched *The Simpsons* together for family fun. At least we were spending time with them in the same room and laughing.

Looking back, Casey said, "Having a picnic in front of the fireplace was one of the most fun things we ever did as a family. I *loved* it."

Blowball power

When Casey was in middle school, she made friends with Vivian Wang, who lived nearby with her sister, parents and grandparents. Going to Vivian's house was like going to little Taiwan. They spoke Mandarin and cooked Taiwanese food.

Vivian spent a lot of time at our house. She often sewed with Casey and me. Vivian's mother complained that Vivian was spending too much time at our house. She didn't trust us much, either. I told my mother about the situation, and she said, "Why should she trust us? Look at the history of white people."

I invited Vivian and her family over for dinner. After homemade pizza, we trooped down to the basement to play *Blowball*. Vivian's mother could

---

How to play Blowball

Blowball is ideal for children's birthday parties, after a family meeting or at an intergenerational event.

Setup: Find a ping pong ball.

Use a ping pong table without a net, or the biggest rectangular table available. Set up a paint can or two other big cans at the edge of the middle of the short ends of the table. All participants kneel on pads on the floor.

To play: Points are scored by blowing the ping pong ball off the opposite side of the table. Nothing can touch the table or ball.

Start the play by pushing the ball from the paint can towards the middle of the table. The only power in the game is breath power. Rotate positions after a few goals.

How to play Spud – a variation on dodge ball.

Setup: play outside in a small or medium size yard. The boundaries can be uneven.

To play: Each person takes a sequential number. To start, a player goes to the middle of the yard, throws up the ball, yells a number, and runs away. The player whose number was called gets the ball as fast as possible and yells "Spud!" Everyone freezes. The ball holder may take three or five steps towards the other players and attempt to hit them with the ball. Players who get hit get a letter – S, P, U or D.

The player who got the letter starts the next round by throwing the ball up and calling someone else's number.

The game ends when a player is hit four times by the ball and spells the word SPUD.

---

hardly blow the ping pong ball because she was laughing so hard at her husband huffing at the ball with all of his might. After we bonded over *Blowball,* Vivian's mother complained less about Vivian's visits to our house.

Solving problems

A family meeting is an ideal venue to solve problems. Living together with anyone requires communication, conflict resolution and crisis management. Not every idea introduced at a family meeting was adopted. Examples include the following.

- I proposed we share inspirational readings at dinner. This never happened.
- When the kids said "shut up" to each other, I proposed and they accepted that they had to put a quarter into a bank, to be donated to charity. This brought attention to the problem and helped abate it. We never donated a single quarter to charity.
- I found this entry: "Kids will cook Sunday (or Saturday). Mom and Dad will do the dishes." This lasted one or two weekends.
- I wanted the children to have a more positive attitude towards cleaning and to clean better. This never changed, but we talked about it and they cleaned regularly. I adjusted my expectations.

Bedtime negotiations

Henry, 9, put bedtime on the family meeting agenda. "I want to stay up later than 8 pm," Henry said, and made a case to his parents.

"What do you have in mind?" said his mother.

"How about 9 o'clock on school nights and 10 pm on weekends?" Henry said, hopefully. "I'm willing to go to 8:30 on weekdays and 9:30 on weekends," said his mother. Henry accepted. Both Henry and his mother were satisfied with the outcome.

Many youths are sleep-deprived because parents take young children out at night and don't set limits so children get sufficient sleep. By the same token, **toddlers don't give up naps, parents do.** Parents must establish good sleep habits for children from birth to age 10 so tweens and teens will be accustomed to getting enough sleep and plan for it.

When children are at day care all day and parents only see them after work, it requires parental discipline to put children to bed early.

It's hard on a child's nervous system to stay up too late. It strains them physically and emotionally because the conversational tone changes after the sun goes down. Parents need time to unwind and have adult conversation and watch R-rated movies without explaining everything to children. Children don't need to be burdened with adult-level conversations and entertainment.

Alison's daughter Kate, 7, went to bed at 9:30 p.m. Alison had to drag her out of bed in the morning on school days. To change the situation, Alison put "Bedtime" on the family meeting agenda.

"Kate, I want you to start going to bed earlier, even if you are just lying in bed reading or looking at books. What time do you think would be reasonable?"

Alison invited Kate to make the first offer in negotiations – a good tactic because children might surprise us.

"How about 8:30?" Kate said.

"No, that's too late. How about in bed by 7:30, lights off by 8 p.m.?" Alison said. Kate agreed.

Kate provided Alison with an alarm clock and taught her how to use it. Kate developed self-reliance by managing her new morning routine, felt more energetic for school because she had sufficient sleep, and Alison had some time at night for adult relationships.

The *What's In It For Me?* factor

Teenagers experience a tug-of-war between the security and innocence of childhood and being free from their family. Teens must often be encouraged to attend family meetings.

If tweens or teen say, "I hate family meetings. I'm not coming. I'm going out with my friends," you might say, "That's up to you. We may decide what jobs you'll do if you're not there."

You could also say, "I hope you come to the family meeting because. I value your input. When would be a good time to schedule the meeting so you can attend?"

It's much easier to convince someone to do something when they have agreed to do so.

Jobs

Use family meetings to divide up household tasks. Invite them to propose ideas and implement them. Here's a record of a family discussion of allocating jobs based on the degree of difficulty.

Hard jobs	Easy Jobs
Kitchen floor	Hall and office
Living room	Dining room
Master bathroom	Powder room
Purple bathroom	Basement steps/hallway
Vacuum upstairs	Vacuum steps
	Wastebaskets

Casey (11): vacuum and dust family room and porch.

Noah (9): vacuum and dust living and dining rooms, steps.

Ian (7): clean purple bathroom, sweep basement steps.

Kris (4): clean powder room, empty garbage cans inside.

If a family only has time for the children to do one chore, doing dinner dishes regularly will suffice. Make it their responsibility. Do not feel sorry for them. Expect them to plan how to get them done, even when they have other things to do. They can learn to work fast as a team. Doing just one job, the dirtier the better, can counteract entitlement.

The power of family meetings

Family meetings teach children myriad skills. Holding them regularly will change the atmosphere in your home. We held family meetings at the kitchen table. Attendance was encouraged, but not required. Beware, those who neglect to attend could get assigned the least-desirable chores.

The earlier a family starts family meetings, the easier it is to gain cooperation and attendance. Hold a meeting for whoever comes. Treats attract attendance. The first family meetings may feel awkward. Some maybe tense. They will not all be perfect.

Commit to have family meetings regularly for a year to establish the tradition. The children will learn to value, use and enjoy them.

Use family meetings as a management tool

As Momager® – family life leader and manager – of three children, we use family meetings every Sunday to plan and manage our family. Bob and I started family meetings within months of our first child's birth. We asked ourselves, "What are we doing?" As our family grew, we reviewed each child's physical, mental and spiritual situation.

The children started coming to family meetings when they had something to say or issues to present. For example, they wanted a raise in allowances and later bedtimes. We suggested they bring a proposal and we would talk about it.

Attendance is optional. They attend if they have something to bring up or they want to hear what we're talking about. They hang around even if they have nothing on the agenda. Sometimes we post it. "Family meeting at 2 p.m." We used to follow an agenda, but the meetings are more free-form today.

With three children (11, 12, 14 years old) and their activities, and my husband and I both employed, there's a lot going on. Family meetings help us communicate and organize our lives. Here are some of the things we do during a family meeting.

- Review how the past week flowed and rate it on a scale of one to ten.
- Look at the scheduling for the coming week
- Solve problems and resolve sibling rivalry as a family
- Plan family vacations
- Work on the family budget
- Review upcoming travel plans for me or my husband
- Talk about the mind-body-spirit connection and how to get to a higher level
- Share a snack – popcorn, chocolate or cookies

Family meetings bond our family and instill confidence in the children. My goal is to have the children learn everything so they can be independent, well-adjusted, loving people who can support themselves and make this world a better place.

I'm supposed to be working my way out of a job. My oldest son, 14, said to me, "Mom, I just need to learn to manage my money a little bit better and learn to drive, and I think I'm ready to move out."

Christine Martinello   The Momager®   Speaker and author

Family meetings are particularly helpful for blended families, multi-generational families, families with long-term visitors such as foreign exchange students and foster children.

Family meetings are one of the most enjoyable and powerful components of a positive parenting plan.

New practice: Hold family meetings twice a month for a year. Allow everyone an opportunity to lead them. Give compliments.

Challenge: Follow-through on agreements made at the meetings in a firm and friendly manner. Take notes.

For discussion or journaling: What are family meetings developing in your children and your family environment? What's working? What could you do to make them work better? What is it like to see your children in the leadership role?

Family meeting tips

- Keep an open agenda posted on the fridge for all family members to write down an agenda item.
- Hold family meetings two to four times a month.
- Encourage everyone to attend by making sure there Is fun, food, something in it for them.
- Be willing to make a decision that impacts someone who has chosen not to attend.
- Rotate the roles of facilitator and scribe.
- Read the minutes aloud from the previous meeting. Keep the minutes as a family legacy.
- Open the meeting by giving compliments to each other.
- Don't try to solve every problem. Airing grievances is helpful. Sometimes children must grow out of a phase.
- Keep the level of problems appropriate for children.

We cannot protect our children from life.
Rudolf Dreikurs

7
Beware of Helicopters

The case of the disabled computer

It was a bleary, chilly rainy October day. The days were getting shorter and colder. The children had transitioned back into the fall school routine. I had the morning alone to write. Hurray.

I logged onto the family computer in my home office. It was 1997, the dawn of the personal computer era and we shared a single computer. At night, the six of us jostled for a turn on AOL to join the latest craze to sweep the nation – e-mail.

I flipped on the marvelous machine, sipped a cup of tea and waited for it to hum to life. And I waited. Nothing happened. Not to worry. I applied the universal fix: shut it off and try again. Still nothing happened, except finally, a blue screen with boxes appeared. I unplugged it and turned it on again. Instead of the blue screen or the fall color palate of orange, green, yellow, brown and red, all I saw was red. Bright red.

Someone had disabled the computer.

Luckily, that someone was safely at middle school. I had a cooling-off period, and time to plan an investigation on the Case of the Disabled Computer.

At 2:20 p.m., Noah, 13, and his siblings ambled home from the bus and opened the fridge for an after-school snack. The dog greeted him warmly.

I skipped saying *Hello.* "Noah, the computer wouldn't turn on this morning. Do you have any idea what's wrong with it?"

"I dunno know." Noah said.

"What did you do last night on the computer?"

"Nothing." Noah sat down to his snack, wondering why my voice had an edge. I was doing my best to follow a positive parenting plan after losing a day of computer use.

"Ian, were you on the computer last night?"

"No, Mom," Ian said. Casey was innocent because she had a piano lesson the night before. The needle of guilt kept pointing to Noah.

"Noah, do you know something I don't know?"

"Well, I *might* have downloaded some music from the Internet," Noah said innocently.

"That shouldn't cause a problem," I said.

"I deleted some files so I'd have more room for music," Noah said so quietly that I could barely hear him.

We eventually discovered that among the deleted files were files that turned on the computer.

"You're lucky you weren't home this morning. I was pretty mad."

"Mmm." Noah quickly retreated to the sanctuary of his room. I didn't follow him or say anything more about the Case of the Disabled Computer. Computers can be repaired and replaced more easily than self-esteem and relationships can be repaired or replaced.

It's usually pointless to get angry, lecture, shame and punish. Nothing could revive the computer. It was never the same again. Noah's actions rendered the machine one megabit from death.

We finally called a professional, Charlie, who charged $400, and revived it to perform like a wounded soldier. It moved slowly, in pain, remembering the trauma of the battlefield.

Bob and I had to reconcile the $400 repair bill. One natural consequence was having no computer for three weeks. The logical consequence was that Noah would repay the $400, by earning the cash.

He would *not* earn the money back by doing extra household chores. We were not a debtors' labor camp.

I felt a pang of guilt for imposing the $400 debt. I thought *Noah didn't know what he was doing to the computer. It was an accident. We have the money.*

Nonetheless, we held Noah accountable for the damage. Some would call us "tough." I agree and disagree. Our decision showed we trusted Noah to solve the problem. The consequence of earning $400 met Jane Nelsen's test of being related, reasonable and respectful.

Other responses to the disabled computer

Instead of holding Noah accountable, we could have done some of the following.

- **Ground Noah for a long time.** This was not necessary because a lack of spending money and no computer naturally restricted him. Grounding him would have bred resentment towards us for being judge, jury and parole officer. We would have had all of the power. Instead, Noah felt empowered by earning the $400.

- **Feel sorry for the Noah** because he had to give up $400 in spending money, and we had the money. The question is, "Who should pay for the mistake: the person who caused it or the person with the most money? The money was coming out of Noah's spending money or mine. Noah caused the problem.

  Families with more dispensable income must be aware of the model of buying solutions to problems, which denies young people the experience that mistakes cost money. It sets up the youths to depend on parents to bail them out, an increasingly expensive habit as young adults create bigger and pricier problems.

- **Pay the $400** to demonstrate "love" and protect him from learning from the pain. This is called helicopter parenting, founded on this mistaken belief, "Noah, we love you so much that we don't trust you to solve this problem."

  Instead, we showed our love by giving him the opportunity to learn from his decision. It was enough rope to burn – and learn – and not enough rope to hang.

A few weeks after Charlie fixed the computer Noah did the same thing and deleted files to make room for more music.

Luckily, Noah was under protective custody at school when I attempted to turn on the disabled machine. At that moment, I understood the meaning of the parental phrase, "I'm going to kill him." Luckily, no child welfare officer, teacher or homeland security officer was in earshot.

I felt a snarl of emotions: pity, guilt and frustration for Noah, topped off with fury. I had a few hours to rein in my emotions. Noah owed us double. He gave me plenty of practice to control my emotions and develop patience.

A surprise bonus

The Case of the Disabled Computer steered the course of Noah's life. I asked Charlie, the computer repairman and friend-of-a-friend, "Would you take on Noah as an indentured servant? He owes us $800 for your bill."

"I could use a strong back. How many nights a week can he work?" Charlie said.

"Let's start with one night a week. I'll bring him to your house and he can go with you on your evening house calls," I said.

"Okay. Bring him tomorrow night at seven. I'll drop him off at the end of the night," Charlie said, initiating a twice-weekly event for several years.

Charlie enjoyed mentoring Noah. The Case of the Disabled Computer had an outcome we never imagined. Noah developed computer repair expertise for life. He earned a bachelor's degree in computer engineering. Computers are his life. Charlie provided him with hands-on training that most of his classmates lacked.

It started with a mistake, and Noah experiencing the related, respectful and reasonable consequence of it. If we had not made him pay, Noah would have missed a life-changing opportunity. He may have still found his way into the computer world, without the wisdom gleaned from scores of house calls with Charlie to fix ailing computers.

When Noah disabled the computer, I didn't ground him. I didn't punish him. I didn't shame him. Hitting him would have been futile and dangerous because he was getting bigger and stronger than me. I felt sorry for him, but not sorry enough to let him off the hook. None of those actions would have restored the computer or created a computer guru.

Consequences differ from *punishment*

Many parents substitute the word "consequence" for "punishment." They believe that it's acceptable to modernize a "punishment" into a "consequence."

Punishment is pain handed down from a higher authority. It includes: grounding, arbitrarily withholding screen time, verbal abuse, criticizing, sarcasm, shaming, blaming and the lowest form of power, hitting the child which says, "The only way I can show I'm more powerful than you is to use my superior size and strength."

These are not consequences. They are punishments. Reward, praise and punishment set up power struggles. When constantly threatened with punishment or criticism, children lose the opportunity to practice making decisions and living with them.

Natural consequences are the best panacea for youngsters to learn from mistakes. They occur with no interference from parents or anyone else. Schools have systems of consequences, which makes it an excellent

---

Money is not the source of all solutions

Jill and Bill have difficulty letting their young adults learn from experience, especially costly experiences. The habit of buying their way out of problems started when they were young and grew bigger and more expensive as the children matured.

"Dad, I'm sorry, but I backed into something and dented the bumper of your new car. I couldn't see it." Cost to dad: $590. Daughter did some office work for dad's business in restitution.

"Mom, I got my license suspended and can't drive. Would you send money for a plane ticket home from college?" Jill sent money for a bus ticket. Cost: $259, plus court and legal fees. Son stacked firewood for a few hours in restitution.

"Dad, I lost my return plane ticket home from Italy. Would you call the airline and get them to issue me another ticket?" Cost: $150 for the new ticket. Daughter agreed to do more office work.

The older the youngsters get, the higher the cost of the bad decisions. Jill and Bill got tired of bailing out their children and began loaning money to the young adults to solve their problems with their own money.

---

place to practice making decisions. The consequences are usually clearly explained, fairly and consistently enforced, and related to behavior.

Here are some examples of reasonable, related, respectful consequences to typical situations at home. Notice the positive phrasing.

- "You may have a ride to Nick's house on Friday night as long as

---

Get the job done with work *and* play

Growing up on a family farm in Loudon, Tennessee in the 1970s, we had a combination of chores and paid jobs. We had not-for-pay chores, such as harvesting garden vegetables, feeding cows, and mowing the lawn.

From age 5, my brothers and I were expected to help with the tobacco farming, which is very labor intensive. We were paid an hourly wage according to our ability that increased as our contributions to the farming operation increased.

Putting tobacco in the barn to dry was a two-person job. My father worked all day and allowed my two brothers and me to take turns helping him. Two of us got to play basketball on a court he had built, while one worked for a while. Then we changed positions. That way, Dad kept us interested and got the work done.

Like most kids, we preferred to play. But I remember watching our parents work much harder than we were asked to work, so it didn't seem like a burden. As I grew older, I remember not liking the tobacco farming business very much. My dad advised me: "If you don't like doing this hard work, then stay focused on getting an education so you can get a good job."

Any job I have had since then has been much easier than farming tobacco, so I have always been highly motivated to contribute at work. My farm experience has helped me stand out among my peers, in school and at work.

I like to tell people, "I'm not smarter or better; I'm just highly motivated." I've managed up to 150 people and am now a senior manager at a Caterpillar dealership.

Howard F. Kirkland, Knoxville, Tennessee

---

the powder room is clean, which you agreed to at the family meeting."

- "People who eat the main course and vegetables may have dessert."
- "No screen time at night until homework is done."
- "Either stay in your room for your nap/quiet time or I will lock the door. The choice is up to you." Follow through kindly and firmly. Young children learn quickly.

The best natural and logical consequences pass the test of the Three Rs, which I hope you have memorized for your positive parenting plan: **related, reasonable and respectful.** If not, it qualifies as punishment and will breed **resentment and revenge**, two Rs to avoid.

Experience is the best teacher

Helicopter parents often avoid punishment, natural or logical consequences, and saying "no." They gravitate to the extreme of protecting a child from experiencing negative ramifications from their actions. Helicopter parents intervene to ensure success. Helicopter parents have never learned to mind their own business and trust the child to make decisions, both good and bad.

When youngsters make decisions and experience the results, they develop self-trust, a foundation for healthy self-esteem. Parents and children will develop mutual respect and healthy boundaries. Youngsters will be empowered to make good decisions when they're teenagers going 60 miles an hour, 60 miles away.

Without opportunities to learn from mistakes, youngsters grow up in a protective bubble. It's a shock when it pops and crashes. A child has no resistance to germs or resilience to handle mistakes. They may constantly turn to their parents to buy and rescue their way out of blunders. Mistakes have provided my best life lessons. Mistakes and failure are learning opportunities. They offer the chance to try again, to try harder, and take a different tack.

Enough rope to burn but not enough to hang

When Arielle, 8, consistently forgot her lunch money, either the school loaned her lunch money or her mother made a special trip to school to deliver the money. Arielle never got an opportunity to learn to feel the result of poor planning.

When her mother nags Arielle every morning, "Do you have your lunch money?" Arielle doesn't learn responsibility and may become mother-deaf. Nothing fatal will happen if Arielle goes hungry for one day. Maybe a friend will loan Arielle some money or share their lunch. Parents perform a disservice by nagging, reminding and rescuing.

Children need the opportunity to feel the consequences of their actions in benign situations. **Taking responsibility will develop self-confidence and good decision making later on.**

Hand writing as a memory tactic

When I have something really important to remember, my son Ian taught me to write it on my hand.

A few years ago, Rotary International sent me to Norway for a month on a Group Study Exchange to foster international goodwill. The names of my Norwegian hosts were often difficult to remember and pronounce. By the time I learned to use their names with confidence – usually about

---

Don't trash my room

Clyde found a related consequence to encourage his teenage daughter Olivia to bring in the empty trash cans from the curb once a week.

"I think we erred in not expecting our two daughters to do more at home. One of the few chores we asked them to do was bring the barrels back to the end of the driveway on trash day when they got home from school.

"After Olivia failed to do it for a couple of weeks in a row, I brought the two empty barrels up to her bedroom so they would be there to greet her when she came home from school. She brought in the barrels for the rest of the school year," Clyde said.

Clyde found a creative consequence. He used action, not words. It was related and somewhat reasonable. It may have violated the rule of respect when he showed Olivia that he meant business.

If you can't change the situation, change your response to it. Cliff changed his response without nagging, yelling, or reminding.

---

three days – it was time to move on to the next host couple. With the write-on-hand system, I used name like "Ingeborg" and "Fridtjof" with confidence on the first day. Hands are very convenient memory joggers.

Children like systems. For example, it can be challenging to remember everything needed for school or a weekend visit at the other parent's home. Children can make checklists, plan ahead and write important things on their hands. Parents can help set up systems and ask children, "Did you check your list?" Take time for training so they can learn to navigate visits.

Ski equipment as a teacher

We took our tribe skiing regularly for six years. Even at age 6, Kristen was responsible to pack her ski bag with socks, mittens, hat, ski boots, ski pants, jacket and anything else, such as a book to read at the lodge. I helped her pack a ski bag in December. It was her job to maintain the system for the winter.

Kristen lived up to the expectation. If something was missing, she borrowed it or improvised. Her ski socks might not have been clean, but she had them. The children carried their own bags and equipment.

We all worked together to pack lunches and load the van. One year we rented a ski house five miles from the mountain. I worked as a ski instructor while Bob was the domo-guru: in charge of making lunch and coordinating the children equipment. Bob did not like it when a child forgot something essential like a pair of boots or skis, which stole a few minutes of his skiing time. The children were not punished for forgetting something, other than Bob's grumbling for missing twenty minutes of skiing.

The children were ages 6 to 13. They lived up to our expectations to be responsible. Many parents at ski areas act like servants to their children by putting on their children's ski boots for them, and lugging the ski equipment while the children skip ahead, empty-handed.

I've heard children ask their parents with an accusing tone, "Did you forget my mittens?" Parents can liberate themselves and say, "I am not your servant." They can encourage and expect children to pull their weight.

Eagles ignore sibling rivalry

The parents of newly hatched bald eagles turn a blind eagle eye towards sibling rivalry. Elder eagles do not interfere if a stronger sibling dominates, even mortally wounds a weaker brother or sister. With this exception, mother and father eagles are literally helicopter parents, hovering over their little chicks. However, they take a passive attitude towards sibling rivalry so the young eagles will be strong. Their survival training starts in the nest by learning to defend against siblings.

Likewise, if human parents constantly intervene in sibling rivalry, no matter what age and gender of the children, they are denying tots-to-teens the opportunity to learn from the natural consequences of their actions.

Sibling rivalry is the problem of the siblings, no matter what the age.

Janine, 8, adored her older brother, Max, 16. She sought his attention and knew how to annoy him to gain it. One day, Max didn't feel like paying Janine any attention. She went into his room and took his iPod. "Look Max, look what I have." Janine flashed the iPod and ran upstairs with Max in pursuit. Max caught up to her and wrenched it out of her hand.

"Ouch, that hurt. Mom, Max hurt me," Janine shouted in pain, so their mother in the kitchen could hear. She began to cry and went to the kitchen so her mother could see how much pain she was in.

Because her mother had joined an online positive parenting group, she didn't interfere. She said, "Janine, I bet that hurt. Maybe next time you'll think twice before you touch something that belongs to Max."

Putting them all in the same boat offers children the opportunity to work out their problems and learn the rules of the world. Some parents are anxious that their children might mortally wound each other if they are allowed to fight. Let them discover that fighting hurts.

Avoid ugly scenes in public

Do you take children out in public, ignoring their bedtime or naptime, expect them to behave, and punish them when they don't?

Do you take children shopping regularly because *you* want to shop, and lose your temper when they misbehave?

Solve the problem by shoring mutual respect. Hire a babysitter or leave them home (with supervision) when you go shopping.

Peace in the car

Quell fighting in the car by stopping the car in a safe place and announcing, "I'll keep driving when you show that you're ready." Such a tactic requires taking a good time for training.

I took time for training before I drove the four children 350 miles to visit my parents. En route to after school activities, if they acted up I immediately stopped the van in a safe place and announced, "I'll keep driving when you tell me you're ready."

By the time we drove on the highway for seven hours, they were able to behave in the car. Stopping the car is related, reasonable and respectful. It puts them all on the same team without blame, punishment or interference.

On the return leg of that trip when I was an hour from home, the children were restless and loud. They needed a break. I handed the map atlas to Casey, 11, and said, "Find a park. They're the green trees on the map." She directed me to a park. I would have rather kept going, but it would have been more stressful and less respectful towards them.

They amused themselves while I took a break, alone, within view, and far enough away to give them freedom to move and play. The last hour of the trip went quickly. We all felt more rested.

Recorded books are an excellent resource. We listened to "The Indian in the Cupboard" read by the author during a twelve-hour trip. Lynne Reid Banks used delightful voices to bring each character alive in our imagination. It's okay to allow children to feel boredom and use their imagination to solve it. Recorded books can mesmerize everyone in the car, including the driver. Listening to one book becomes a family activity, versus the children being amused by TV and computer games.

The control factor

An effective way to teach good decision-making is to allow children to make age-appropriate choices and experience the natural and logical consequence, without interference. Freedom is one of human's most cherished values, and contributes significantly to human happiness.

In his book, *The Pursuit of Happiness, Who is Happy and Why*, David P. Myers describes examples of people who find happiness as nursing home patients, welfare recipients, students, living in communist regimes, and under apartheid in South Africa. Myers found that the common denominator to happy people, regardless of income and education, is **more control yields more happiness.**

It may seem harsh for Noah to have earned $800 in restitution; to let a child or teen fail at school; to allow a child to go hungry at lunchtime. In each instance, the child has control of the situation.

Parents can offer children choices – both acceptable to the parent – to empower children make decisions. Like adults, children and teens will sometimes make bad decisions. One of the most loving things parents can do is to avoid the helicopter and allow youngsters to experience the results of their decisions.

It's sometimes difficult to say "no" or to watch a loved one suffer when you could rescue them. Noah remembers that he disabled the computer twice, but has no memory of earning the $800.

Cooking rice makes a lasting impression

My childhood job from about 8 years old onwards was to wash and cook the rice. We had an electric rice cooker, so there was no risk of burning it. My mother taught me how to measure the rice from the large bag of rice we kept in the pantry, put it in the rice pot, check for anything strange, like bugs, rinse it, measure the water, and make sure the lid was on tight, and plug it in and start it.

There were a lot of steps, but it was an easy job for me. It taught me about responsibility and the importance of following through on a task.

Once I rushed because I was making the rice during commercial breaks of a TV show. When it was time to eat, we discovered I had not pressed the button to start the cooking. Dinner was late, and it was my fault. My family forgave me, but I never made the mistake again. More than 20 years later in 2009, I always check that the little red light is on.

I learned to finish what I start. Consequences, even at a young age, help shape our ability to make good judgment. In business as in life, making good decisions are crucial to success. Actions have consequences.

Vicki Yip   Beijing, China
Partner--KismetGiftshop.com

Using natural and logical consequences takes time and planning. It is more instructive and respectful than reward and punishment. Influencing children's behavior by bribery and manipulation teaches a child to behave when there's something in it for them.

It's more challenging to find time for training when both parents are employed full-time and if children are distracted with activity-mania. Slowing down the pace of life reduces stress and gives parents and children more time together. Finding time for children to experience consequences and focus on doing a few chores requires discipline, determination and decompression that can't be bought in a bottle.

Using natural and logical consequences contributes to a child's self-esteem. When children are allowed to learn life's lessons without harsh punishment, the child feels respected. It contributes to a child's dignity, which translates into self-esteem, according to research by Nathaniel Branden.

New practice: Be kind and firm when employing natural and logical consequences that are related, reasonable and respectful.

Challenge: Give up manipulating your children's behavior with unrelated threats. Invest the time and creativity to set up natural and logical consequences to minimize resentment and revenge.

For discussion or journaling: How did your parents teach you about the world? What did that create in you? Describe your favorite teacher. What techniques did that person use to influence you?

Key points from Beware of Helicopters

- The best teachers are natural consequences which happen without interference.
- Keep logical consequences related, respectful and reasonable
- Instead of threatening punishment, agree on boundaries in advance.
- Have a positive parenting plan ready so you can control your emotions and avoid anger.
- Give children enough rope to burn but not enough to hang.
- Take a good time for training when necessary.
- Expect children to manage most of the details of their lives, especially at school.
- With practice, you can learn to say nothing when you're aching to say, "I told you so." Eventually, silence will come naturally.
- Natural and logical consequences promote mutual respect and give children permission to make mistakes and learn from them.
- Children will develop good decision making that comes in handy when they become teens and they are 60 miles away going 60 miles an hour.

How to begin to raise a child? First rule: leave him alone.
Second rule: leave him alone. Third rule: leave him alone.
D.H. Lawrence

8
Sound Familiar?

When Noah broke the family computer, it was mostly *my* problem, not Noah's. Not having a computer to work on for several weeks impacted my life far more than Noah's. However, he caused the problem, so he helped solve it.

The foundation to a healthy relationship is to establish mutual respect by asking, "Whose problem is it?" By stepping back and offering encouragement, parents will empower children to learn to make good decisions.

Here are some typical scenarios to determine who owns problems you may be facing because many parenting challenges are universal. The goal is for parents to define their responsibilities and encourage children to handle their problems.

Children leave belongings in living areas

For younger children, it's the parents' problem when children leave their belongings in living areas because parents care about the condition of the room.

For older children, leaving belongings in living areas can be the child's problem if she can't find something because it got lost, thrown away, or a parent has put it away or temporarily confiscated it.

Natural or logical consequence

Parents of younger must take time for training and expect to pick up toys with children for years. Don't have more toys than there is room to store them. If there are too many toys, give some away. Limit the quantity. Rotate toys to storage areas. It's fun to bring forgotten toys out again.

Asking a young child to clean a messy room is like asking an adult to clean up K-Mart. Where to start? Provide children a cubby or crate near the entrance of the home for personal belongings.

Put "picking up" on the family meeting agenda. Brainstorm solutions. For chronic offenders, create a box for lost or confiscated belongings. The youth can negotiate for return of item.

My children each had a crate by the door for backpacks, shoes and personal items. If I wanted the room neat, I tossed errant belongings into their crates. Every few months, I asked them to clean them out.

There was a hole in the family room floor to vent heat from the furnace. I loosened the vent and put a box under it to catch for lost and found belongings. Sometimes an object went into "the box," stayed there for a few months and was not missed. Important objects were quickly claimed by their owners. It was helpful they knew where to look.

Occasionally I had to pick out my socks or shoes from the box. It was related, reasonable and hilarious when mom's stuff ended up down in the basement. The box cultivated some low-key revenge because we all enjoyed dropping things down the vent. The room was cleaner as a result, with less talking and more action.

Clean K-Mart?

Telling someone less than 11 years old – to "clean your room," is like telling an adult to cleanup K-Mart. Where would to start on such an overwhelming task? Children up to age 10 or 12 are not able to independently tackle the task of "cleaning your room." Even tweens and teens can occasionally use help to clean their room. Do it with them. Don't nag or expect that they children can clean their rooms independently to high standards.

Moderate screen time and electronics

Monitoring access to electronics is the parents' problem. It could become a major problem if the youth develops an addiction and electronics replace other activities, such as outdoor play time, human interaction and reading.

Establish a nightly bedtime routine of reading aloud to toddlers. Advance to picture books, to easy readers and novels. Continue reading aloud at night through fifth grade, which will hopefully make them lifelong readers. It will also make bedtime go more smoothly.

After a bath and a book, bed feels awfully good. Start a bedtime reading routine if your child is still in elementary school. If you don't know any good read-aloud novels, ask a children's librarian or go to a bookstore. I loved the Roald Dahl easy readers such as *James and the Giant Peach*. We read aloud the *Little House on the Prairie* series by Laura Ingalls Wilder to our boys and girls, as well as the *Chronicles of Narnia* series by C.S. Lewis.

Parents are the antidote to screen time

Be aware if you are contributing to an abundance of sugared screen time by your children. Lazy parents feed the addiction by habitually turning on a movie to mesmerize children, and bring hand-held electronic games everywhere with a child to placate him.

Take a different tack. Expect your child to think creatively and entertain himself in the car, while waiting in line and for appointments or visiting people. Suggest they bring a book. Hopefully they're in the habit of always have a book going and a pile of books from the library.

Avoid placating a child with your cell phone while waiting because you're making the cell phone an object of value, increasing the interest and robbing them of an opportunity to use the gray matter between their ears to hum a tune, invent an imaginary friend, or say the alphabet backwards.

Do not buy video games until they beg for them. Even then, require that they save some of their "own" money for them. Don't rush into such purchases. They can learn to live without possessions their friends have and find alternative entertainment.

Talk with other parents about how they handle electronics in their home. Experiment with options besides setting time limits on screen time

"If we put a limit on the time they can play on the computer, they might play more," Scott said of his two daughters, ages 10 and 8. Their family prefers give-and-take with no rigid structure around computer time.

Other parents may have ideas to copy or tweak. There is no right age for a child to have a cell phone. However, they must demonstrate the responsibility to take care of it. If the cell phone is for parents' benefit to better hover over the children, don't get it.

Tweens and teens can use cell phones to lie and mislead parents about their whereabouts. Cell phones can also be used to keep a parent in service

---

A feasible *brain drain* policy

Pete and his wife Janet of Milwaukee have figured out a respectful reasonable family computer use policy.

"My 17-year-old daughter would like nothing better than to spend her spare time on *Facebook*. My 15-year-old son would like nothing better than to play *War Craft* all day and all night. My 12-year-old daughter would like nothing better than to watch Disney channel movies online, without limit," Pete said.

Pete and Janet forbid "brain drain" (TV and computer use) on weeknights. The computer can only be used for homework. Each child is allowed five hours of self-regulated "brain drain" on weekends, with spot checks by Pete and Janet.

"At first, we used a timer to track each computer user to control the 'brain drain.' It didn't work because they beat the system," said Pete, a computer programmer.

"Now, we have no formal system to track their five hours of weekend screen time. When Janet and I do a spot check and catch them violating the agreement, they are banned from using the computer for a multiple number of hours as a consequence, which they know about in advance so they don't risk it."

The family considers TVs and computers equal "brain drains," and keeps them in the family room where they can be monitored. The children are not permitted to have "brain drains" in bedrooms.

"Some of our friends have asked, 'Do the adults have to abide by the same rules?' Of course not. We can regulate our own 'brain drain' time," Pete said. It is reasonable for parents to have different rules than children.

If the children complain, Pete says, "Life isn't fair. Deal with it."

---

to youngsters because it eliminates the need to plan ahead. "Come and get me now," can become the standard operating procedure, and create entitlement.

Depending on the maturity of the youngster, most can handle a cell phone by high school, and it is useful for parents. With the proliferation of text messaging and electronic bullying, taking away a cell phone could be called reasonable, related and respectful. Life will go on without a cell phone.

Suggestions to moderate screen time

Use family meetings to negotiate use of electronics. Teach and model moderation in your own lives. Talk about how you control your desires and addictions.

Parents can control use of electronics until children are 10 or 11 years old. From then on, parents must collaborate with youngsters to make good decisions on how to spend their time. Avoid the role of computer cop. Occasional "spot checks" are more effective.

Educate youngsters over age 11 on the dangers of addiction by sharing stories, books and movies about addictive behavior. Parents are responsible to moderate child's access to computers and TV. Negotiate a reasonable amount of screen time allowed each day and enforce it.

I recommend one hour a day of screen time. Sixty minutes in front of a computer, TV or electronic game is sufficient. Keep all electronics in common areas within sight of the kitchen so youngsters are not sequestered in their rooms with electronics.

Plan activities with other families

- Host a musicale. Invite families whose members play musical instruments and like to sing. Their skills can range from beginners to professional. Post a signup list for children and adults to play (not perform) their favorite songs. Encourage impromptu combos to form. It's okay to rehearse on stage. Be an enthusiastic audience.

- Host a play reading party. Pick a play from the library. Assign roles to children and adults. Change halfway through. You don't have to read the whole thing.

- Host a pot luck dinner or order pizza and show a family movie.

- Go camping. It's always more fun with other families.

- Go sledding, to the beach, canoeing, to the corner park to play Frisbee or a pickup soccer or baseball game. Get outside and get moving. It's always more fun with other families.

Natural and logical consequences

When a child refuses to do what a parent wants or violates an agreement, parents sometimes deny access to electronics as a punishment. Avoid the temptation to manipulate a child's behavior by controlling access to screen time at unrelated times.

At a restaurant while waiting for the food to be served, Dan, 8, spoke too loudly and provoked his younger brother. Dad said, "Stop it now or no PlayStation for the rest of the week."

Such action qualifies as punishment. Denying use of the PlayStation has no relevance to eating in a restaurant. Dad shows a lack of a positive parenting plan when he manipulates Dan's behavior by denying use of the game.

The natural consequence of acting up in a restaurant is to leave immediately and eat at home. It is inconvenient for parents, but taking time for training will teach the child to live up to your expectations and behave in public.

Taking kind and firm action works better than pleas, counting and threats of unrelated punishment. Taking action demonstrates you mean business. **Remember, when a consequence is related, reasonable and respectful, it minimizes revenge and resentment.**

Toddlers can choose to stay in bed

If my toddlers were newly out of a crib and tempted to wander, I offered a choice: "Either stay in your bedroom or I will shut the door and you will not be able to open it." Both choices were acceptable to me. We used plastic doorknob covers to prevent children from opening doors, when necessary, for their safety and our peace of mind. We rarely had to shut the door to contain them if they were not able to choose to stay in bed.

Beth hadn't considered offering Joey the option of staying in bed until she learned about a positive parenting plan. She put Joey in the decision-making seat. He learned self-control and to live with the consequences of his choices.

"It only took a few nights. The first few nights, Joey screamed and I felt guilty, but I couldn't stand him running around the house every night. After a few nights, he decided to stay in bed without us closing the door. We had peace," Beth said. She gave Joey a reasonable and respectful choice related to his behavior that kept him safe and literally allowed his parents to sleep at night.

Child repeatedly acts up in class

Parents and children share the problem of misbehaving at school because if a child gets expelled, it becomes a family problem.

Natural or logical consequence

Parents must investigate the unconscious goals for the youngster's behavior described in Chapter 17, *Name it and tame it.*

Perhaps the child feels deeply discouraged, in which case the tonic is encouragement.

The child may be desperate out for one on one time with a parent. Set up a weekly date with the child and have special time together, as simple as taking a walk or playing ping pong. It's unnecessary to spend a lot of money or take a special excursion. He may need more daily encouragement from you. Believe in your child and expect more from him.

> ## The soggy potato chip law
> Ideally, we all would like a nice fresh crisp potato chip from the top of the bag.
> However, when a fresh potato chip is not available, we'll take a soggy potato chip because it's better than nothing.
> Likewise with children. Attention for bad behavior is better than being ignored.
> Aim to give fresh crisp potato chips regularly through positive attention and encouragement.

School behavior problems may have myriad causes. A youngster might unconsciously be reinforcing negative relationships with peers and teachers. He may gain negative attention or feel powerful by failing a class or a grade. School may not be a pleasant and safe place for the student. The problem might be too big for the child to handle. Parents may transfer the student to another school or seek professional help. Start with encouragement and spending more time with the child.

Homework harmony

Typical children in third grade and older can be responsible for doing homework at a time of their choosing, or not.

Imagine how you would feel if you came home from a long day of work at 6 p.m., and found your boss waiting in your kitchen. She towers over you by a foot (she's a former basketball star) and declares: "You have to finish the last fifteen minutes of that project *now*. And what about that report that's due next week? I want you to start it right now. I don't care if you're tired or hungry. Now is the time to do it, so I don't have to worry that you'll get it done. No whining, either. I'm the boss."

Natural or logical consequence

Parents of typical children and those with special needs, learning disabilities and attention disorders can allow the child to take the lead in doing homework and asking for help because **homework is the child's problem.**

"He'll never do it," Barb said about Nathan, 10, diagnosed with ADHD. Instead of nagging him, they can use a family meeting to create agreements on how and when he will do his homework.

Barb can ask Nathan once a day, "What time did you agree to do your homework? "Do you need help?" Barb can set limits and enforce their agreements. If homework has become a battleground and threatens to sour their relationship, Barb can take a step back. Nathan can decide whether or not to complete homework assignments and experience the consequences at school. Another option is to agree that there's no screen time until homework is done.

Let homework be a child's problem. They can handle it. Let go of the problem and put the child in the driver's seat. School is a safe place for children to experience natural and logical consequences of their choices so they can learn to make decisions and live with the outcome.

Child dawdles in the morning before daycare

Parents need to get to work on time so it is their problem to establish a morning routine to manage their child's behavior.

Natural or logical consequence

Parents discuss the problem at a family meeting and ask for suggestions. If the child can write, ask her to make a "morning checklist" to post in the kitchen. A parent can also make the list. Teach her how to read the clock, use a timer and give warnings, such as, "We're leaving in five minutes. What do you need to do to get ready?"

Analyze the child's behavior in terms of the four goals of behavior in Chapter 17. Ask yourself, "Am I giving the child enough positive attention so she does not have to seek the soggy potato chip?"

Notice when they are ready on time and encourage them: "It makes it easier to get going in the morning when you're ready. Thanks."

Invest in spending special time with them. Slow down and carve out five to fifteen minutes to be with them with no agenda every day. Include them in making and cleaning up dinner. Being depended upon to set the table or load the dishwasher creates a sense of importance and family connection. Set aside time before bed every night for a relaxing bedtime routine of bath, book and singing.

Avoid the temptation of using guilt or adult logic such as, "If mommy doesn't get to work on time, mommy can't earn money to buy food and toys for you." Children under age 6 have not reached the age of reason. It's the parents' problem to arrive at work on time and stay employed. Parents can form a positive plan for the family to be ready on time in the morning without bribery, star charts, praise, manipulation logic or punishment.

Set up a routine that works. Take time for training to ensure they comply. If they choose not to comply, agree on a consequence that is related, respectful and reasonable to avoid resentment and revenge. If necessary, choose a good time for training. When the child is not ready, take them to day care or school while still in their pajamas. Get in the car whether they're ready or not.

Messy bedrooms

Give children autonomy to keep their room any way they want. It shows mutual respect and allows them to experience the consequences of their choices. The condition of their room does not impact parents, unless parents let it bother them. It's an opportunity to practice letting go.

My children opted to keep their rooms messy. As a result it was difficult to open the door; distinguish clean clothes from dirty; and to find the floor and walk on it. They started doing their own laundry when too many clean clothes ended up in the laundry basket.

I stepped around the detritus and practiced keeping quiet. When they're interested, let them choose how to paint their rooms. It gives them an opportunity to experiment, develop judgment and self-trust.

Natural or logical consequence

They can experience the consequences of having friends over to a messy room. You can walk around the stuff or avoid going in and occasionally offer to help clean it up.

If your family hires a cleaning service, allow children to decide whether or not to partake of the luxury. Experiencing the work of cleaning their own room will help them appreciate a cleaning service if you hire one.

Whose pet is it?

Three of Samantha's five children, ages 9, 7 and 6, agreed to take care of their rabbits. They loathed cleaning the cage.

When Brittany, 8, the most consistent cage-cleaner, broke her foot and

---

The comfort of bedtime routines

Children crave routines that adults might find boring. Bob and I spent about a decade eating family dinner followed by a bedtime routine.

"Do you want dishes or bath?" I asked Bob, who inevitably chose "bath," which was fine with me. I enjoyed the Zen of doing dishes alone because I had been with the children all day.

A warm bath is a relaxing way to end the day. Mental institutions use baths to calm patients down. My gang took a bath together until they got too big to fit into the tub. A thorough rub-down and tooth-brushing followed, topped off with reading or storytelling while lying on the child's bed. If she was in a crib, we lied on our bed together or held her, read and sang.

The bedtime ritual works by going slowly and without interruptions from phone calls or other distractions. Drugged by the warm bath, book and undivided attention, the child has no option but to slip into dreamland. Our children stayed in bed. They did not come begging for more attention or soggy potato chips. We invested in the time before bed, and satiated their emotional needs.

---

couldn't clean the cage, Samantha got fed up with the smell from the cage and nagging the children to clean it. The odor was Samantha's problem. Pushing the limits of parental patience can be a good because it clarifies the family's values.

Natural and logical consequence

"I told the kids that I was tired of listening to them complain about the bunnies and if they didn't come up with a solution I was going to place an ad to find a new home for them," Samantha said. This put all of the children in the same boat and gave them an excellent opportunity to solve a problem together.

"After trying to get me involved in their argument, they discussed it among themselves and came up with a solution. They now switch off the chores when the seasons change, four times a year. They've stopped complaining because they know the alternative is to not have the bunnies any more. It makes life so much easier. I love that they came up with the solution." Samantha said.

Cleaning the bunnies' cage is everyone's problem. Having bunnies is a privilege. Samantha was willing to take action and give away the bunnies as a related, reasonable and respectful consequence when they neglect to clean the cage.

Chores and consequences develop responsibility

The majority of the 560 respondents from age 11 to age 92 who took my survey on childhood chores agreed that **doing childhood chores developed responsibility in them.**

Those who did chores were more likely to do well at school and not get involved in serious high school substance abuse. Chores develop self-discipline, which translates into making good independent decisions.

When youngsters learn to live with the ramifications of their decisions, they develop resilience and self-trust. **The goal is to establish a positive parent-child relationship before adolescence** by eliminating criticism, nagging and punishment. It takes time to allow natural consequences to occur. It takes effort and patience to set up logical consequences. Noah took at least six months to pay back the $800.

We live in an instant messaging-disposable culture where we're quick to throw away anything that doesn't bring immediate gratification. We have little patience if a marriage or job becomes too challenging. Parenting is a long-term investment. Hang in there.

Early practice prevents problems

Determining ownership of problems and allowing children **enough rope to burn but not enough to hang** will develop good decision making in them. You want them to make good decisions when they're teens, 60 miles away going 60 miles an hour. Their lives will depend on it.

This book is intended for parents of tots-to-teens. Learn about adolescence so you can prepare, not despair for teenagers. I hope you're motivated to take action **now** with a positive parenting plan to prevent problems **later.**

Before they become teens, provide ample practice in solving problems

---

Whose problem is chores?

Parents want the lawn mowed, bathrooms cleaned and table set.

Some families are able to set up an expectation that children pitch in without being asked. Youngsters in a perfect world will work willingly, without reminding, do their regular chores.

You're thinking *It's not a perfect world.* Because most of us don't live on farms and children don't see the direct impact of their contributions, parents must learn finesse to persuade children to contribute to the household, without threats, bribery or punishment.

Suggestions for parents

Develop a personal authority based on kindness and firmness.

Do not give up and do the job for youngsters because it's easier than following through.

Set up a system at a family meeting with the children's agreement. Detach from the consequence if a child chooses to procrastinate.

Choose a good time for training and implementing respectful, related and reasonable natural or logical consequences.

Have faith that childhood chores will develop responsibility. You are making a worthwhile investment in their future. Parenting is for the energetic and strong.

---

and managing their time, bedroom, schoolwork and relationships without constant adult interference.

New practice: Ask "Whose problem is it?" before you take responsibility or intervene.

Challenge: Choose one chronic situation, step back and allow your child to own the problem. Use action, not words. If you must say something in a difficult situation, make it encouraging. Discuss it a family meeting. **Let go of the outcome.**

For discussion or journaling: Reflect on your childhood and how you learned a significant lesson without your parents' interference.

Key points from *Sound Familiar?*

- Negotiate and enforce boundaries around screen time. Hold children to their agreements with kindness and firmness.
- Model moderation in pursuit of your passions.
- Notice how you use electronics as a babysitter or to entertain children. Expect them to unplug more often, think creatively and play outdoors.
- Talk with other parents about how to regulate screen time. Regularly read aloud to children through elementary school.
- Occasionally organize activities with other families such as musicales, sledding, canoeing, camping, potlucks or going to a park.
- Minimize activity-mania. Allow unstructured time for exploration, quiet time and chores.
- Trust that students can manage their schoolwork from third grade onwards.
- Give children the freedom to choose when to do homework and what condition to keep their room.
- Pet care is the pet owner's responsibility, within reason, and the child's age.

Nature teaches us to be ... Nature can teach you being.
Eckhart Tolle

9
When it Rains, Stomp Barefoot in Puddles

M y parents discovered tent camping in 1970 after my brother Danny and his gang of teenage friends pooled their money to buy a tent at Gaylord's Department Store in Wilmington, Delaware. My parents were paying college tuition for at least two of us when they realized camping promoted three values: frugality, family time and freedom to travel.

The chores of camping and the exposure to the elements didn't detract from the benefits or deter my parents. On the contrary, camping delighted them. My parents could see the country without paying for motels or eating out.

Camping allows families to spend time together, work together as a team to set up and break camp, cook, gather firewood, fetch water, and engage with nature. Because children are naturally grounded in the present moment, they appreciate the beauty of dew hanging precariously on a cobweb in the morning, the gurgle of a stream and huge rocks to explore. Nature accepts the cycle of life and death. Nature is constantly changing while being in the present moment. Nature is simple and connected to the earth, weather and sky. Death and decay bestow new life in the woods.

Studies of people in hospitals, housing projects and schools have discovered that connection to nature – as simple as seeing a tree outside of a window – makes a significant difference in their quality of life.

No way to camping? Try day trips

Not everyone is able to surrender the dirt, chaos, chores, cold/heat, bugs, beasts, unpredictability and dampness of camping. If camping is out of the question, connect with nature regularly through short jaunts in nearby open space. Taking a family walk for an hour or two is a start.

Immersing in nature in a park or conservation land is like a drug. Walk slowly, with no agenda, ready to stop when something beckons. If it starts to rain, button up and pull on your hood. Let loose a little Get wet and muddy. Wear old clothes and leave the electronics at home. If you don't have a dog, borrow one because a dog improves a walk in the woods like chocolate sauce improves ice cream.

Our first dog Boomer inspired me to discover a network of trails in our town that is typical of many New England communities. Most of the trails started from roads we had driven on for several years. Finding the trail system existed a few feet away was like slipping through the wardrobe in Narnia. We entered a magical world full of trees, wildflowers, deer tracks, abandoned cars, foxes, raccoons, skunks and birds.

Take all day or part of a day to visit a nearby state park or conservation area. Pack a lunch. Be open to what Eckhart Tolle calls the sacredness of nature. Slow down and open to what nature can teach us about being still, listening, looking, smelling and touching. Take a few minutes to connect to the earth.

Follow your children's lead in exploring the simple beauty of a flower, the rough texture of a rock, the glorious feeling of mud. Follow the scent of wild grapes. Stop to pick wild berries. Pick up a stick and use it for walking. Find a narrow branch to swat away bugs. Revel in the stillness, quiet beauty and cycle of life.

The rain in Maine is relentless

Tent camping is my preferred way to take a dose of nature with its unpredictability and wildness. My parents and their youngest four children experienced a baptism by Maine rain on our first two-week camping trip.

Rain poured on Danny's canvas tent on the first night of a much-anticipated trip to the foreign state of Maine. We had driven more than 500 mile, a very long way by 1970 standards, to be greeted by rain.

Maine rain trumped my parents' stalwartness. They surrendered and took the six of us out for dinner, an extravagance reserved for special occasions. We returned from a lobster dinner to the saggy, soggy tent to play "Oh Hell," a lengthy group card game that involves psychology, risk, luck, and laughter.

The game starts by dealing one card to everyone. At the next deal, two cards are dealt to everyone, then three cards, and so on until all of the deck is dealt. The dealer then starts subtracting one card each round, down to dealing a final round of one card for every player.

Every deal, players bid the number of tricks they predict they will win. The number of tricks bid must be either greater or less than the number of cards dealt. The dealer bids last and must make the bid for available tricks either too high or too low if it isn't already, so a player is forced to lose. One play keeps score and tracks the number of cards dealt. **It takes a very long time to play "Oh Hell."**

I cherish the memory of the Rain in Maine, with endless rounds of "Oh Hell" under the dim light of a Coleman lantern while rain fought its way into our sanctuary.

"Don't touch the canvas!" my parents said repeatedly, to keep more water from seeping in. The toilets were a hundred yards away, through the dark and rain. I didn't care. It was fun. We were safe, fed, warm, damp, together and laughing in spite of everything.

The rain smelled clean amid the pine woods. I relished the feeling of cold puddles sloshing around in my flip flops on the way to the bathhouse. Having grown up in a city, the air and water in Maine were the most pristine I had ever experienced.

The day after the storm, our gear was so wet my parents surrendered again and checked into a motel to dry out. The motel was sanitized, safe and dry compared to the campground

To this day, I savor the clean, moist earthy smell on a moonless rainstorm in the woods. I love the sensation of walking at night in a light mist, surrounded by the bouquet of pine, the soothing sound of water slipping from trees, and the taste of the rain on my lips. Packing the car, setting up the tent, cooking outside, fetching water and firewood and breaking camp were adventures. From a child's perspective, camping never felt like a chore. It was a family adventure.

A change in perspective

Fast forward fifteen years and my attitude shifted when I became the mother camping in the rain with four damp and dirty little bodies. There's work involved in camping. I realized my parents might not have liked "Oh Hell" very much. They might have preferred to have been playing bridge with friends in a dry well-lit living room while we watched TV in the next room.

My parents could've taken a morose attitude towards the rain. They dealt with the rain in Maine the same way they dealt with nine children – with a stalwart attitude, sense of humor and few complaints.

Every time our family told the story of the rain in Maine, I re-lived it with them and added details. It is an unforgettable chapter in our family nostalgia. This is why blended families benefit from the bonding experience of camping.

My parents' attitude reflected their life strategy: Face problems head-on with a positive outlook. Morning will come. The sun and a Laundromat will dry you out. Bacon, eggs and toast cooked over an open fire, eaten at a damp picnic table, flavored with errant pine needles, tastes ten times better than in a warm kitchen under a shingled roof.

Camping makes people appreciate the comforts of home and the beauty of nature. Camping was a glorious adventure, which included work willingly shared by all.

After the rain in Maine, my father bought a new Eureka tent, renowned for protection against the elements and promptly sealed all of the tent seams of the bucket-bottom. We appreciated the technology of that tent. One camping strategy is to buy one piece of new equipment every summer. Invest in warm sleeping bags.

Today's families are not as adventuresome or willing to do the work of camping. Some families relegate camping to the men, sons and scouts. This sexism divides the family on weekends and reinforces the belief that females should stay clean, pretty and, somewhat boring.

To enjoy camping, one must surrender to the fact that children get instantly dirty and wet from socks to hat. If it's raining and warm out, put on a bathing suit and stomp in the puddles. Wear flip flops and walk in the rain. It's only water. It can only go as far as the skin. Camping gives children open-ended time to discover wild blackberries, snakes, frogs, creeks and nature. That's therapeutic in itself. One must slow down and enjoy the Zen of work in living outdoors.

Blended families can bond in the woods

I recommend an annual weekend camping trip for all families, especially blended ones. Ignore their protests and leave the electronics at home. Require people to be present with each other in nature

Blended families must hope for adversity while camping, the more the better to initiate the new family. Parents must model stalwartness and teamwork, and expect the children to copy them. Let them complain because it will unite children and be the first chapter of the new family's nostalgia.

A family is not created on good times when the going is easy. Family bonds get sealed on moonless, rainy, windy nights, holed up in a wet tent, powerless against the elements, saying and playing "Oh Hell." Everyone will retell the story for years and laugh about the suffering -- later.

Develop a campy attitude at home

Imagine allowing your children and teens to live life as though they're camping and can't get out of the rain. View challenges of weather, dirt and wildlife as learning opportunities.

Allow them to experience the natural and logical consequences of their decisions. I guarantee they will develop judgment and learn from the consequences of those decisions, much more powerfully than through parental nagging, warning or rescue.

I'm not suggesting that parents create difficult situations or withhold guidance and assistance. Life challenges emerge naturally in the woods and at home. Camping allows children to practice meeting challenges with stalwartness. Children will observe and copy what they see their parents do. They pay particular attention to actions over words.

Offer quiet confidence in their ability to solve problems. "That's a tough one. I bet you can figure out a solution. I have faith in you." Saying nothing and giving freedom build confidence.

Ask questions: "Do you have a plan? Do you need help? What do you think?" Provide encouragement: "It takes courage to try again. I bet you can do it. Do you have any ideas on how you can do it differently this time?" Difficult experiences build character and resilience. If we protect our children from them, we deny them learning opportunities and the opportunity to practice making decisions in life.

We survived Hurricane Bob in the wilderness

Camping in the rain in the wilderness baptized our family when the children were between ages 3 and 10. Six months ahead, Bob and I had planned a two-week canoe-camping adventure in the Maine wilderness. Bob and I never paid much attention to weather forecasts.

Because the children were young, we had arranged for a motorboat to deliver us 10 miles to a remote camping site on the northern edge of a big lake. The plan was to take day trips from there and be picked up three days later.

As we loaded the boat with the meticulously chosen supplies, someone on the boat launch said, "How about that hurricane coming up the coast?"

Bob and I exchanged a glance. We were young and energetic. No hurricane would interfere with our expedition. We continued to load the boat silently, because turning back was not an option.

The campsite was idyllic, woodsy and remote. We set up two tents and a rain fly, just in case. The torrential Maine rain started that night and abated thirty hours later. The dampness caused a chill in the air and bones.

The best strategy was to sit in the tent together and invent diversions like heating up water under the dining fly for hot drinks, playing "Oh Hell" and "Uno." I learned to tie knots from the directions that happened to come with the clothesline packed in the gear. I still use some of the knots learned on that trip.

The first time I dared to look at my watch, hoping it was lunchtime, it was 9:30 a.m. The next time I looked at my watch, hoping it was dinnertime, it was 2:30 p.m. We surrendered to the situation, laughed as much as possible, and tried in vain to stay warm and dry. There was no one to call in that pre-cell phone era. There were enjoyable aspects to the trip. What doesn't kill you makes you stronger.

Rain, the character builder

Opportunities for stalwartness can be found at home by facing the elements. When I coached a girl's middle school recreational soccer team, one Saturday only five of the ten players showed up because of injuries and other commitments. A broken wrist had sidelined my daughter Casey.

Our opponent was the top team in the six-versus-six league. They had ten players against our five.

In an act of sportsmanship that will always be remembered, Coach Manny Battista removed one of his players from the field to make a fairer match of five-on-five. His gesture was a candle in the wind. Or should I say "a candle in the rain," because around halftime, the heavens opened and it poured.

My five girls played the entire game without a substitute. When Manny called "Sub, ref!" rain and sweat dripped down my girls' foreheads while they silently watched a fresh lineup of five players prance onto the field, rested and ready, chatting, and high-fiving their replacements.

The 30-second substitution breaks provided the only rest my team had on that soggy day. The other team racked up so many goals that we lost count. We did not concede.

A miracle happened in the fourth quarter. One of our players scored a goal. I think the other team had lost focus. No matter. It was a legitimate goal. The girls leapt with joy, and congratulated each other like they had just won a gold medal.

The next week we had a full roster with substitutes and sunshine. The game was so much easier and our spirits soared. We had come together as a team during the muddy wet defeat.

At the end of the season, we were the come-from-behind surprise victors of the league playoff.

The second-ranked team had scored an upset victory when it beat the top-ranked team, which had beaten us in the rain.

In last round of the playoffs, we came from behind and scored a goal late in the fourth-quarter to win. I believe one of the reasons we won was because the rain taught us to keep going no matter what, and we had bonded in the mud and defeat.

That's stalwartness.

Survival skills inspired boy scouting

Robert Baden-Powell, a lieutenant-general in the British Army, recognized the power of camping to develop character. He started the Boy Scout movement in 1893 because he realized that young recruits lacked wilderness survival skills.

Here are quotes from Baden-Powell, published in an old interview.

"When these young fellows joined the Army, they had learned reading, writing and arithmetic in school, but as a rule, not much else. They were nice lads and made very good parade soldiers, obeyed orders, kept themselves clean and smart and all that, but they had never been taught to be men, how to look after themselves, and so on.

"...They had been brought up in the herd at school, they were trained as a herd in the Army. They simply did as they were told and had no ideas or initiative of their own. In action, they carried out orders, but if their officer was shot, they were as helpless as a flock of sheep. Tell one of them to ride out alone with a message on a dark night and ten-to-one, he would lose his way.

"I wanted to make them feel that they were a match for any enemy, able to find their way by the stars or map, accustomed to notice all tracks and signs to read their meaning, and able to fend for themselves, away from regimental cooks and barracks. I wanted them to have courage, from confidence in themselves and a sense of duty; I wanted them to have knowledge of how to cook their own grub; in short, I wanted each man to be an efficient, all-round reliable individual.

"The scheme worked. The men loved the training and Scouting became very popular in the regiment."

Baden-Powell gave his men opportunities to develop decision-making, judgment and initiative, independently. They were expected to solve problems and learn to survive in the wilderness. I like Baden-Powell's goal: "I wanted each man to be an efficient, all-around reliable individual."

Camping provides that opportunity.

Stalwartness begins at home

Children learn stalwartness when parents encourage them to show up to do jobs or play on a team when it's inconvenient, wet, or they don't feel like it.

Encouraging tots-to-teens to try again after failure, teaches stalwartness and self-discipline. **Self-discipline is the motivation to make your self do something hard. It is a prerequisite for success in life.**

It is a great mistake to arrange your child's life to avoid failure and adversity. Experience is the best teacher. When we feel something from a life lesson, usually pain or regret, we have an opportunity to learn from it. If we never feel pain, there is no motivation to change. We will only expect the world to be our servant.

Lifelong relationships require people to be able to survive, to be stalwart: dependable, loyal, sturdy and strong, no matter what. Camping in the rain teaches us to have hope for tomorrow.

New practice: Model stalwartness. Encourage tots-to-teens to develop self-discipline. Explore nearby patches of nature as a family on a day trip.

Challenge: Go camping for a long weekend with your family at least once a year without electronics. Have fun, no matter what the weather, and model courage in the face of adversity. Play "Oh Hell."

For discussion or journaling: Describe the vacations your family went on together. How did your parents handle adversity? What did those times create in you?

Key points from When it Rains, Stomp Barefoot in Puddles

- An annual camping trip is recommended for typical families and especially for blended families.
- Blended families must hope for things to go wrong when camping. The worse things get, the stronger the bond.
- Slow down and enjoy the chores of setting up camp, cooking outdoors, getting water and firewood and breaking camp.
- Camping is more fun with other families. Arrange annual excursions.
- If camping is not for you, go on day trips or half-day trips.
- Insist ALL electronics be left at home.
- Laugh loudly and compete equally with your children at "Uno" and "Oh Hell."

*Nothing would be more tiresome than eating and drinking if
God had not made them a pleasure as well as a necessity.*
Voltaire

10
Family dinner:
The Glue for Your Crew

In a scene of *Martian Child* (New Line Cinema 2007) actor John Cusack adopts a 6-year-old Martian boy, serves him a grilled cheese sandwich, and says, "I enjoyed grilled cheese sandwiches when I was your age."

With a single sandwich on the table, Cusack sits beside the boy and tries to convince him to eat. They push the plate back and forth. The boy ultimately refuses the food.

In a later scene, the extended family gathers and the children are set up to eat at a separate table while adults eat at the main table.

The lack of a family meal in "Martian Child" subtly reinforces the modern practice to feed children "kid food" separately.

Imagine if Cusack made himself a grilled cheese sandwich – with some adult ingredients to jazz it up, such as gourmet cheese and a tomato. Cusack could set a completely different dynamic by taking a bite and saying, "My father used to make me grilled cheese sandwiches. This is delicious. How's yours?"

Making the time and effort to eat together sets a different table than when children and adults eat separately.

One of the most significant findings of my survey was that teens who reported eating family dinner three times or more a week were nearly three times less likely to report serious high school substance abuse. **Family dinner is an anti-drug** because it cuts in half the time from after school and bedtime that teens have to get into mischief.

My research showed that teenagers eat family dinner less often ironically when they need it more often to reinforce family values and keep them out of trouble. Eating dinner together provides an opportunity to be with your teens. **They don't have to like it. They just have to do it.**

Survey respondents of all ages reported that when they were teens, the rate of sharing a family dinner dropped by twenty points.

For the sake of family dinner, parents may have to insist teens schedule their lives to eat dinner with them. Parents may have to sacrifice gourmet food, business dinners, and getting together with friends. If you have children, make time for them – especially dinnertime.

Many studies affirm the benefits of family dinner. Researchers at Ohio State University found that family meals, adequate sleep and limited weekday TV viewing correlate with slimmer children. The National Center on Addiction and Substance Abuse at Columbia University reported that the more frequently youths share a family dinner, the less likely they will smoke, use drugs or drink. Young people in their study said they prefer to eat dinner with their parents.

My survey showed a correlation between doing chores and family dinners. Respondents who had family dinner regularly were 1.2 times more likely to have done chores. Family dinner is the glue for your crew, and its repercussions will echo for years.

Family dinner is worth prioritizing

The daily task of fixing dinner is relentless and sometimes thankless. I cooked for three to seven people daily for twenty-five years. It is a skill, a responsibility and is a time-honored ritual worth practicing.

Eating with young children requires patience. It teaches them to belong to a family, sit still for the meal, and interact with each other.

Cheese curls and a video for dinner

Some families view cooking and cleaning up as a detested chore that steals time instead of giving time together.

"My stepmom HATES to cook," said Christina Ammon, whose parents divorced when she was 4 years old in 1978. Ammon grew up with her father, stepmother, two half-brothers and step-sister. Her parents either picked up fast-food for dinner or gave the children a few bucks to forage at the corner store for chips and candy, to be consumed while reading the newspaper and watching videos in separate rooms.

"I envied my friends' families who shared nice meals together. I felt lonely and sad about the way our family was. I think it profoundly affected our sense of being a family. A lot is shared around a dinner table -- jokes, stories, and just the mundane happenings of the day. I honestly don't feel like I know my siblings. We spent little time together. We were independent and spent a lot of time with our own friends," she said.

A few tImes a year, Ammon's family prepared and ate a meal together. "Thanksgiving was very stressful for my stepmom, even when it was just instant potatoes and frozen turkey tidbits. It sent her into a frenzy. But once we sat down, I really did enjoy it, though I remember feeling a little shy about talking in front of everyone and sharing stories. I was not used to talking in front of everyone," Ammon said.

Visits to friends' homes provided an experience of how other families shared meals together. "I liked to eat at other people's houses. My best friend's mother loved to cook. It seemed like an enormous production that took lots of time. Her family seemed to have lots of inside jokes and nicknames for each other. They shared a closeness and levity that was absent in my family," she said.

Ammon's unconventional family gave her the ability to fend for herself.

"I gained independence. I definitely know how to be alone, and I'm very self-sufficient. My grandmother said that as a young child, I dragged a chair into the kitchen to reach the bowls and cereal to make myself breakfast," she said.

After graduating from college, Ammon worked on an organic farm where she discovered the miracle of growing things, the alchemy of cooking from scratch and sharing a delicious meal prepared together.

Christina Ammon, writer, Ashland, Oregon--www.christina-ammon.com

I understand that people would rather avoid family dinner, and many do. My survey showed the Millennials eat dinner much less than their predecessors. Between the generations, the frequency of sharing a family dinner dropped by twenty points. Of those 21 and older, 83 percent ate dinner together three or more times a week when they were growing up.

Of those between 11 and 18 years old, only 62 percent shared a family dinner three or more times a week. A twenty-point drop is significant. At this rate, the next generation will be eating dinner in the car, in front of a screen, or skipping it entirely because of the time and energy required.

Roadblocks to family dinner include activity-mania, the fast pace of our world, and the economic necessity for both parents to work outside of the home. Parents must summon the energy at the end of the day to cook a healthy meal quickly, amidst dueling obligations. Don't fall prey to the easy road. You'll miss out on a family-builder.

Here are comments about family dinner from people who responded to my survey.

- 13-year-old girl: "Sometimes I'm not in the mood, but I almost always have fun catching up with my family."
- 57-year-old woman: "It was good when parents were talking; we played word games after dinner and I loved that."
- 30-year-old woman: "Didn't really think much about it as it was happening, but looking back, I think it's one of the things that have kept us close as a family even through some tough times."

When you set the table and room with care and treat your children with mutual respect, family dinner – or breakfast – has the power to bond your family, instill values and teach manners and the art of conversation.

How wonderful that refueling our bodies is so pleasant. How wonderful that the joy of eating multiplies when done with other people. How wonderful the earth provides a variety of foods to enjoy.

Many of my happiest memories growing up are connected to the ritual of cooking and eating together – for sustenance and celebration. **Lessons learned around the family dinner table can stick for a lifetime.**

In the 1800s and early 1900s, it was a privilege for children to eat dinner with adults. Children of wealthy families were required to eat in the pantry with the servants until they mastered manners and the art of conversation Family dinner is THE place for parents to embed values into children, and reinforce them with the pleasure of food and each others' company while breaking in half the time teens have to make poor choices...

Family time is prime time

Our culture emphasizes that **work** is the priority, instead of **families**. Companies that offer flextime allow parents to better fulfill family responsibilities. People with children are often more efficient at work because they want to finish and get home to their families.

If a company doesn't offer flextime, an employed couple can ask for a family-friendly schedule. Working 25, 30 or 35 hours a week opens up time during the week to handle medical appointments, children's activities and preparing family dinners.

Being a parent requires quantity and quality time. Open-ended time is needed to luxuriate in a walk together on a fall day. Unrushed time to make cookies together, to drive together to weekly music lessons, to build a birdhouse in the basement, read a story, tell a story or joke and make dinner.

One parent can opt to stay at home as a domo-guru. One parent can opt to work at a less demanding career so s/he can come home earlier in the day, or at least come home at 3, 4 or 5 p.m. One parent can set up his/her career to work from home and be available for children's needs and to start dinner at 4 p.m.

Companies and organizations that offer flextime give a gift to employees who have children at home. The option to start work early and leave by 3 or 4 p.m. is a tremendous advantage to a family. Companies that offer flextime may develop loyal employees among parents. Managing two careers and children is one of the challenges of the new millennium. We must institute new systems and expectations for employees with children.

When we don't prioritize children, our families, marriages and society will eventually pay the price one way or another. Troubled children and fraying marriages distract employees. Healthy families and marriages need an investment of time and attention.

Plan dinner in the morning

My mother advised, **"Think about dinner in the morning,"** a practice that makes it easier to cook every night. Planning dinner in the morning allows time to defrost food, buy a missing ingredient, or to start a step early in the day.

Take that advice one step further for parents who juggle outside employment with children's activities: **think about dinner the night before.**

Coming home from work late in the day without a plan is a major roadblock to a family dinner.

When I have a plan and the ingredients on hand, I can prepare dinner in less time than it takes to eat out. If I get home at 5:30 or 6 p.m. with no plan, I waste precious time assessing what's on hand, looking up recipes, and defrosting ingredients in the microwave.

Having a mental plan makes it easier to pull together a respectable family dinner in thirty minutes, which is faster than eating out. I count on my family's help. Involving younger children is an investment in a future cook.

People who take family dinner time seriously plan ahead. Either leave a note or call from work to remind a youngster at home to make the pizza dough after school, boil the beans, or put the chicken in the oven. Better yet, plan the week's meals on the weekend and post them.

Invite your children to start to cook, either with you or independently. Support their efforts by buying ingredients they need, offering guidance, appreciating what they make, and not complaining about the mess.

Everything is reinforced at dinnertime – values, storytelling and humor, consideration for others, establishing traditions and more. Family dinner is the glue that holds together your crew.

If you don't eat together regularly, start with **one** family meal per week, either dinner or breakfast with everyone involved in the preparation. Talk about anything. Look at each other. Love each other. Ask questions and then listen. Tell stories and jokes – that show your insecurities, success and failures. Eating dinner together regularly will pay off in myriad ways.

New practice: Set the goal of eating a family meal at dinner or breakfast two to five times a week, if you don't already do so.

Challenge: Involve the children in meal preparation and cleanup.

For discussion or journaling: What changes do you need to make in my lifestyle to make family dinner a priority?

Key points from Family Dinner, The Glue for Your Crew

- Take the time and make the effort for family dinners. They are an investment in your family life.
- Family dinner is a rich venue to learn social skills, bond, tell stories and share values.
- Plan ahead and cook simple dinners. Involve the children in menu planning, shopping, preparation and cleanup.
- Not every family dinner will be peaceful and perfect.
- Family dinners teach young children how to sit still for a meal and enjoy being together.
- Family dinners keep a strong connection to teens and tweens even though they may resist. Insist over their resistance.

Don't worry that children never listen to you;
worry that they are always watching you.
Robert Fulghum

11

I am not your friend.
Set Boundaries

What would a river be like without a shoreline? Flooded and out of control.

Where would the United States be without its borders between Canada and Mexico? Confused. Conflicted. Chaotic. Tri-lingual.

Where would you be if your mother shared your bedroom right now? Crazy.

No matter what your relationship with your mother, imagine how intrusive it would be to have her invade your bedroom, office, briefcase, purse or home. You might respond by getting angry, running away or keeping secrets and lying.

A woman said to a co-worker, "I told my son I want to be his best friend."

The woman's goal is unrealistic and inappropriate, regardless of her son's age. Say her son is 13. Will she play video games and baseball with him? Will she snicker about female anatomy with him? Will she talk with him about menopause?

Appropriate boundaries are respectful. Parents must avoid the temptation to befriend their children. It blurs the parent-child boundary and undermines the goal of developing a resilient adult who is able to live independently. Parents must avoid being their children's friend or servant. Appropriate boundaries to ensure the child feels safe and are vital to a positive parenting plan.

Most parents fall into two categories: saying "no" too little, or saying "no" too much. Parents who say "no" too little abdicate their parental duty and may cultivate entitlement, risky behavior and irresponsibility.

Tots-to-teens may feel insecure about boundaries that are too strong or too weak. They may eat the wrong foods, not get enough sleep, experiment with drugs and alcohol and engage in risky behavior.

At the other end of the spectrum, parents may over-flex their power and impose unreasonable limits, which invite rebellion, resentment and deceit from children. **Both extremes are not healthy.**

Boundaries teach respect for natural laws

No one is exempt from rules of the physical world and laws. I make decisions every day to avoid:

- a reckless automobile or skiing accident;
- speeding tickets;
- addiction to drugs, alcohol or food;
- stealing, murder and adultery;
- getting fired from a job;
- drowning; and
- hurting a friend's feelings.

Fear and a respect for the consequences of my decisions influence my daily choices even though I drive and ski cautiously while sometimes going fast, I practice moderation when eating and drinking; abstain from drugs; avoid stealing/killing people/extra-marital affairs; I am an excellent swimmer, and have many friends.

To develop the ability to make good independent decisions, I want to be in my child's conscience asking, "What would Mom say if I did that?"

I give them enough rope to burn, but not enough to hang. As they get older, they go up the escalator of decision-making. The higher they go on the escalator, the more independent decisions they make, and live with the outcome.

Authoritarian parents who verbally or physically abuse children can create bullies, liars and rebels. If mom or dad is a nag or a tyrant, the young person may dismiss parental influence and escape by removing themselves physically or emotionally.

If Mom or Dad has merged with the child as "best friends," it denies the child his or her own identity and the opportunity to develop judgment.

Take the case of Laura, 30, an only child who talks on the phone with

---

Chores set an internal compass

Starting when I was 8 years old in 1986 until I left home, my sister and I did chores every single Saturday of our life. There were times I wanted to spend the night at my friend's house on Friday and the only way I would be allowed is if I came home the next morning to do chores.

Back then, I hated it, but now that I am an adult I realize the reasons for it. Even when I was 3 years old, I had to clean up any mess I made. I had to put back any toy I took out when I finished playing with it.

It has helped me to keep my home clean and tidy on a daily basis; keep my appointments; and keep my word with things I say I will do.

I believe that having to put away my toys has kept me focused because *I had to do it.* As a business owner, I have daily tasks to get done – and I do get them done.

In 2007, I created *Sobo*, short for soul and body, fitness for the soul, body and mind. It is a fun, dance exercise program that incorporates positive thinking and personal development.

Jillian Montes   Hobe Sound, Florida   www.SoboFitness.com

both of her parents daily. "I have trouble making even simple decisions, like what dress to buy," said Laura. She is an example of having too few boundaries and some aspects of her development are stunted.

Instead of rebelling or cutting off her parents, Laura accepts the stifling relationship. The situation comes with a cost: the inability to make decisions; and a benefit: a close relationship with her parents. The wild card is how Laura's life mate will reconcile the over-dependence on her parents.

By adolescence, the results of a dozen years of limit-setting – or lack thereof, become evident. By college, youths who have been either over- or under-regulated by parents may act out with reckless, dangerous and expensive abandon.

It's critical for parents to set appropriate limits. Parents must:
- avoid befriending their children;
- say NO appropriately so the child feels safe and loved;
- associate LOVE, not guilt, with the word NO;
- associate the development of responsibility and self-discipline with the word NO;
- be caring and firm when setting limits; and
- negotiate appropriate boundaries with tots-to-teenagers.

Use action instead of words

Gina has three girls, 19, 15, and 12 who grew up with nannies while Gina and her husband operated a computer company.

Gina is adamant. "I am not their friend. That is not my job. My job is to be their mother. I've never felt guilty about my children being in day care. When we're home, we're home, and I'm there as a parent. I'm not there as a friend. I've told them from the get-go, *I'm not your friend, I'm your mother.*"

Gina sets a simple goal for her children: "I want people to like you and to want you to come over to visit. I have been known to grab their little face up and say, *That is enough,*" she said.

When parents take time for training and set limits, it establishes basic expectations for behavior – both in the house and outside.

"When Isabella was 4 and her younger sister was 1 year old, we were at a department store. She started throwing a super-tantrum in the middle of the store. We took her outside and said, *You will not act like that in a store.*

144

We let her calm down and went back in and she was fine, Gina said. Gina illustrates how to set respectful limits. When a child acts up at a store or restaurant, the natural consequence is to leave. Immediately. And maybe not go back.

Another option is to sit with the child in the car for a time. Parents can also show respect for children by hiring babysitters to avoid dragging children on long shopping trips.

While on vacation when our children were ages 3 to 10, we spent a long day exploring and had planned to treat them to dinner at a restaurant. While settling down and looking at the menu, the children began squabbling. It was clear they did not have the emotional energy to behave properly at a restaurant.

Even though Bob and I did not feel like cooking, we left the restaurant, went back to the cabin and prepared boxed macaroni and cheese, because it was all we had on hand, and put them to bed as soon as possible. It required time and energy when we didn't feel like it, and staying in the restaurant was a not viable choice.

Guardrails provide security

Imagine the biggest bridge you can think of, like the Tappan Zee Bridge over the Hudson River in New York or the Golden Gate Bridge in San Francisco. Imagine driving towards the crest of the bridge, over an ice-cold, deep, sprawling channel below.

Now, imagine there are no guardrails.

Think how terrifying it would feel to not have guardrails while going over the bridge.

When was the last time you hit a guardrail on a bridge?

You've probably never hit a guardrail on a bridge. Just knowing they are there provides a feeling of security.

Setting limits operate the same way as guardrails on a bridge. They create an atmosphere of safety. There's no need to feel guilty about setting a guardrail by saying "no."

Tots-to-teens depend on parents to be the guardrails.

Give choices approved by you

The key to negotiating limits and giving choices is that both options are acceptable to the parent. As children develop self-control, it's up to parents to set limits and partner with the child to self-regulate. Here are some examples.

"You can have two or three marshmallows."

"You can walk or ride your bike to your friend's house."

"Here's $75 to spend on school clothes."

"You can clean the bathroom anytime, as long as it's done by Friday."

"You have one hour of screen time a day."

"You can eat breakfast after you are dressed," said to a toddler.

It's critical to involve children in setting boundaries, because they feel more in control and are more likely to abide by the decision. Both choices are always acceptable to the parents, and enforced the by parent in a firm and friendly manner.

Master the art of sitting quietly

While sitting in a one-hour church service designed to include children, Morgan, 5, use colored pencils kept in a plastic cup. Every time Morgan returned a pencil to the cup, the sound echoed loudly in the sanctuary. His mother Amy said, "Stop. Shh. That's too noisy." He put another pencil back in the cup and it rattled loudly.

Amy attempted to take away the pencils. Morgan protested and threatened a temper tantrum. His mother sighed and allowed Morgan to continue his disruptive behavior. Morgan and his older brother declined the invitation for children to gather in the front for a story. They climbed under the pews and lied on the floor. Unwilling to add to the disturbance, Amy did nothing to stop them.

Morgan is still young enough that he doesn't have the option to stay home from church alone. Morgan can learn appropriate behavior if Amy gives one quiet and firm warning: "You must put the pencils back quietly or you may not have them."

Amy must take away the pencils if he continues. If Morgan has a tantrum, she has to take time for training, without anger, and take him outside until he is ready to return and behave appropriately. The training will be a good investment because Amy said, "I have trouble taking my children places in public."

At home, Amy must take time for training and set limits kindly and firmly. Morgan and his brother will learn that Amy will give one warning and take action without words, negotiation or explanation. **Children will learn to respond to limits that are set respectfully and consistently and fairly enforced.**

Amy can use family meetings to talk about appropriate behavior when they're in public. She will have to take time for training when the children are out in public and at an activity they enjoy. She must give one warning and take them home in a firm and friendly manner, without giving in to belated promises of, "I'll be good."

Strategy: Timed work sessions

My father's philosophy was: "Keep children busy with purpose-filled work and they won't have time to get into trouble." It worked. As the father of five children I've seen the same results with my own kids. Even their employers have thanked me.

My children are ages 10, 11, 13, 18, and 20. They have all helped with the care, training, and showing of our horses. We also have raised lambs, chickens, dogs, and done our share of gardening.

My wife and I tell them what is expected, show them how to accomplish the task, watch them while they work on their own, correct things when necessary, and then thank them for doing a good job.

All of them clean their rooms, put away their laundry and do dishes. Heavy cleaning days are twice a week or so (bathrooms, sweeping). Yard work and laundry are about once a week.

Many of the duties are time-controlled. My wife will set a timer and say, "For the next fifteen minutes everyone has to help in the kitchen." We all work well together, and the children, who are home-schooled, seem to take it all in stride.

Timothy Palla   McDermott, Ohio

Telephone manners

How a child answers the family telephone is an indicator of family boundaries. Some parents give children the right to screen parents' phone calls, which are not the child's business.

From the farm to the firm

I grew up on my family's 220-acre dairy farm in Wisconsin. From a young age I had chores around the farm, as well as chores around the house such as dusting and vacuuming. I helped my father and brother by washing and preparing the cows for milking. I fed the cows and calves, cleaned the barn, painted fences, raked hay in the fields and mowed the lawn – a four hour endeavor.

From age 10, I was paid $5/hour for my farm work. I diligently kept track of my hours and submitted them to my parents for cash.

From an early age, I had the sense I was part of a team. My parents and two older brothers all worked together on the farm. Both of my grandfathers would help out by driving tractors, planting crops, and mowing hay. I liked that I was able to contribute and do things alongside of my brothers. It gave me a sense of responsibility at an early age. I learned to take pride in my work.

I remember sometimes having to forego opportunities for fun because of my responsibilities. For example, one summer I wasn't able to play in volleyball league with my friends because we didn't get done milking in time for me to get to the games.

I believe that my childhood experience instilled within me a strong work ethic and sense of responsibility that carried into my career. In 2004 at age 28 I started my own marketing and design agency. I have ten people working for me. In 2006, the chamber of commerce recognized us as a *Rising Star* company in northeastern Wisconsin. In 2009, we were named "Wisconsin's Emerging Small Business of the Year."

Michelle Richard   Appleton, Wisconsin
www.coalescemarketing.com

When I called, 15-year-old Kaitlin said, "Who's this?" in a tone that said "It's my business to know who calls my father," whom she lives alone with because her mother is dead.

I answered, "Susan," knowing there are hundreds of Susans in the world. Sometimes I'll say, "Gina Obama," because parents' phone calls are not a child's business.

Parents can invent a hundred excuses why it's okay for children to invade their privacy. Children don't need to know everything. They are not our friends; they are our children. We take responsibility for them. It is **not** a relationship of equals, even though we aspire to have a democratic home environment.

Parents owe children privacy in their phone calls and friendships, backpacks, school life and bedrooms. When I served on the PTA at my daughter's kindergarten center school, we discussed how to get a PTA notice home to the parents via children's backpacks.

"I go right for Margo's backpack every day as soon as she gets home," said Nicole, another mother.

How would Nicole feel if her daughter grabbed her purse and went through it when she got home? It's inappropriate. It denies Margo the opportunity to learn to give school notices to Nicole. Margo needs to be the conduit between her school life and parents for school business.

Over time, the invasion of privacy could teach Margo to lie to protect herself from an intrusive mother. It could establish a pattern that will make it difficult to have a healthy adult-to-adult relationship. **Respectful boundaries are fundamental to long-term relationships.**

Encourage independence

It is the duty of parents to render ourselves obsolete. Any relationship with children after age 18 is optional. Some children opt to leave home sooner and create a potentially volatile situation. From birth, a baby is on the "up" escalator, headed towards independence. Every single day, they need us less and less.

The harder parents try to hold on, circle above and interfere, the more annoying it is to the children. Parents who do too much for children deny them the opportunity to learn life skills.

Parents unconsciously send this message: "I can't trust you to take care of yourself or make decisions for your well-being." Parents can create co-dependency if they: handle all of the child's domestic chores such as cooking, cleaning and laundry; meddle with difficult relationships; "snoopervise" homework; and how they spend allowances. Many young people are ill-prepared to leave home or make good independent choices.

The challenge for single parents

It is a greater challenge for single parents to set boundaries. It's lonely without another adult in the house. Children are convenient and inappropriate "friends" for single parents.

Take the case of Bill and Jenna, divorced parents who live 1,000 miles apart, and share custody of Meghan, 5. Here are some examples of how Bill violated healthy parent-child boundaries.

Bill said to Meghan on the phone, "I'm going to the hospital next week for some tests, but don't you worry. Daddy's going to be okay. I'm not going to die."

Meghan said to Jenna, "My dad says that you're going to court, and you have lawyers, and we're going to get this all straightened out."

Jenna said, "During dinner, my husband and I were talking about the cost of something and Meghan said, 'Why are you breaking my Dad? You have more money than he has.'"

Jenna asked, "What do you mean, Meghan?"

"My dad knows," Meghan said, and started to cry.

Meghan does not need to be privy to information about her father's health, custody battles or money. It is the parents' responsibility to keep life normal and worry-free for children.

Like many single parents, Bill could benefit by developing adult friendships and free his daughter from adult problems and friendship. Bill is not alone in befriending his 5-year-old daughter. Single parents face a particular challenge to avoid emotional incest, especially if they have only one child.

Mike, 6, is the only child of Liz, a single mother. Mike spends three days a week and every-other-weekend with his father. When Mike is with his mother, she treats Mike like the sun around which she revolves. Both parents compete for Mike's attention.

Physically, mentally and emotionally, Liz views Mike like an equal or gives him more rights than her. Liz often acts as his servant and has difficulty setting boundaries for Mike, such as getting him to bed on time.

"I like having him around," Liz said.

Dreikurs would call this a case of undue attention. Others would call it emotional enmeshment. It is critical for Liz to establish respectful boundaries and train Mike to expect reasonable amounts of attention. Parents and children are not meant to be friends and equals.

Enmeshment between a mother and son may explode when the boy reaches puberty and realizes, *I could never have sex with my mother.* The party is over. He may respond by boxing her out of his life, a natural response to emotional incest.

Childhood enmeshment with a parent may set the stage for difficult relationships with the opposite sex when the child grows up, according to marriage and family therapist Jan Bergstrom. Parents must set and enforce appropriate emotional boundaries, and let children be children. Adults have the obligation to find adult friends, and not befriend their children.

Setting limits prepares children for school

When a child enters kindergarten, teachers notice if boundaries are set and enforced at home. Lack of boundaries and chaos translate into a child with no internal compass, and a harbinger of future trouble.

"Jonathan is making me crazy," said Mary Beth, a kindergarten teacher in October. "Jonathan has no idea what the word 'no' means. I've talked with his mother and she has no desire to change."

When a child like Jonathan shows up at school, the teacher has a difficult task -- to create a safe range of behavior for the child, with no support from home.

"Jonathan takes so much attention for me to constantly set limits for him that it cheats the rest of the class, because they know how to follow directions. I'm exhausted by the end of the day. I don't think his mother ever said 'no' to him," said Mary Beth wearily.

Jonathan is an extreme example. Without limits or encountering the rules of the world, Jonathan could make some potentially lethal decisions as a teenager.

Be the guardrails on the bridge

You may be thinking, "Doesn't this contradict the previous rigmarole about creating a democratic home with mutual respect and family meetings?"

Yes and no. Children and parents are not equals. Parents are the family leaders who involve children in age-appropriate decisions, and respect the child's rights. No one is entitled to too many or too few rights in a family. No one ought to act as the family's servant or dictator. Find moderation by setting guardrails.

Appropriate boundaries create security for children. Discipline, teaching a child about the world, can be a positive parenting plan and include encouragement, family meetings, household chores, and allowing youngsters to discover the rules of the world through natural and logical consequences.

Teaching children about the world does not have to break their spirit. Instead, it gives their children a safe container in which to thrive. Children do not need parents as friends. They parents as teachers and mentors. Members of the original "Me Generation" of Baby Boomers are reluctant to set limits and have created the "Me-Me-Me Generation," according to author and researcher Jean Twenge, Ph.D., author of *Generation Me*.

The "Me-Me-Me" generation is so self-absorbed and accustomed to parents being in their service, it's difficult to leave home and separate from parents after such a childhood, according to Twenge.

Healthy boundaries, like guardrails on a bridge, set the stage for a positive lifelong relationship, and give children confidence to navigate live on their own, and to make good independent decisions when parents are not around.

New practice: Set boundaries that are respectful, reasonable and reflect the children's maturity. Invite input at family meetings and negotiate. They'll be more likely to abide by boundaries they co-create.

Challenge: If you have violated healthy boundaries, begin establishing guardrails around your privacy and theirs. Seek professional help if needed.

For discussion or journaling: What kind of parent are you – one with too many limits or too few? What has this developed in your child? What makes it hard for you to say "no" or "yes"?

Key points from *I am not your friend.*

- Parents who say "no" too little abdicate the responsibility to set boundaries, which provide a feeling of security for tots-to-teens.

- Too few boundaries may cultivate entitlement, insecurity, risky behavior and irresponsibility.

- Parents who say "no" too much may cultivate a no-win power struggle, rebellion and risky behavior.

- Negotiate boundaries with youngsters. Let them make the first proposal. It could be better than what you had in mind.

- Single parents need to make adult friends and not rely on children as friends. It is inappropriate and unfair to the children.

- Consistency, kindness and firmness are the foundation to healthy boundaries.

If you want children to keep their feet on the ground,
put some responsibility on their shoulders.
Abigail Van Buren

12
Self-excess-teem
and Entitlement

A t age 13, my son Ian said, "I'm going to build a skateboard ramp in the driveway."

"Okay," I said, and thinking, *We'll see if he gets started. If he does, we may have to help him finish. We can always have a bonfire.*

Ian built a skateboard ramp in our driveway with scant help from Bob or me, fueled by a decade of simple regular chores, encouragement, family meetings, mutual respect and natural and logical consequences.

By the way, Ian was a difficult toddler with whom I often engaged in power struggles. His stalwartness drove me parenting classes.

Ian, now 25, offered the following reflection on the skateboard ramp project.

Ian and the skateboard ramp

It was the summer of my thirteenth year. My friend Joe loaned me the plans to build a quarter-pipe ramp. Joe was an in-line skater, which skateboarders look down upon.

The directions were only two pages long and came with three pictures. I looked at the pictures the same way I looked at the pictures on Lego™ boxes, which come with easy instructions on how to build what is in the picture. On the other sides of the boxes were cool versions of spaceships, castles, or pirate ships, with no directions on how to build them.

My brother Noah and I deduced that they wouldn't have put the pictures on the box if you couldn't build it with what's in the box. Legos™ gave me practice building things from pictures.

I paid $300 for the wood and materials with money I had saved from babysitting, working at Denali's Bakery, and as a bag-boy at a grocery store. After my mother took me to buy supplies, the hardest part was getting started, which my friend Steve helped me to do. He was excited at the prospect of having a ramp to ride his BMX bike on.

I figured I could build a ramp that was taller than me at age 13 because of building Legos™ and building with Dad. I figured Dad would help me if I got really stuck.

When I got to the problem of how to cut a circular shape from three-quarter inch plywood, Mom gave me Tom Teller's telephone number and said, "He's an engineer, a smart guy. Maybe he can help."

I called and Mr. Teller came over and showed me how to scribe the quarter circle that forms the outer edges of the ramp. It's called a "quarter pipe" because the profile of the ramp is one-quarter of a circle.

The skateboard ramp plans were incomplete. They didn't tell me how to join to pieces of plywood or how to connect the ramp with the deck. I was stumped a number of times because the plans stank. But a couple of eight-inch bolts solved most of my problems.

In the end, the ramp worked, and I used it a ton.

It taught me a number of valuable lessons about where supports are needed and how to frame. Steve helped quite a bit. I didn't let Steve use the circular saw, even though he was a year older. I didn't trust him to not saw his finger off. The ramp lasted quite a while, and had a second life on my friend Marc's tennis court until we destroyed it, beam-by-beam. It was sturdy and hard to take down.

The power of encouragement

Here's a review on the difference between praise and encouragement, with the goal to avoid self-excess-teem, a self-belief built upon false pretense. Praise is the first impulse of many parents: "I'm so proud of you for building such a beautiful ramp." The problem with praise is it is reserved

---

Farm chores teach management skills

From the time I was 5 years old in 1951, one of my chores on the 200 acres my family farmed in Nebraska was to help feed the farm hands. I picked vegetables, fed calves, collected eggs, picked corn from the fields and pulled weeds. Four of us lived in a three-room house, so we had to be organized there, too.

In later years, my mom said, "I know you had to work too hard on the farm, but we didn't have any choice."

At the time I hated it. And, it instilled in me values and principles that have served me in life, and as the basis for a thirty-year career as an organizing and productivity consultant.

When I had children, I noticed that my friends struggled to "get their act together" and manage motherhood, I think because they didn't have parents like mine. I continue to use lessons I learned on the farm.

My dad used to say, "Half of any job is having the right tool. Since 1978, I have taught small business owners how to choose and use the right tools to create a profitable, sustainable business.

Barbara Hemphill   Raleigh, North Carolina
www.PaperTigerInstitute.com

---

for the completion of the project, when little courage is needed. Ian needed courage to conceive of the idea, to begin, and when he faced problems. Little courage is required at the end.

Praise is given upon completion, for success. Praise focuses on the doer and how it reflects on the parents. Praise fuels the ego and pride and is reserved for accomplishment.

Encouragement is a specific observation about what's going on, offered before, during and after an activity. En**courage**ment gives courage when someone is making an effort or trying again after failure.

Here are examples of encouragement I offered for the skateboard ramp.

"That corner looks tricky. How did you get it straight?"

"The foundation feels sturdy."

"What's that crossbeam for?"

"It's starting to look like a skateboard ramp."

"How will you make the wood to bend on the ramp?"

"It might rain today – remember to put away Dad's tools."

Open-ended question also worked, such as, "How is it coming?"

Saying nothing.

I practiced encouragement by staying out of his way; acting like a consultant; driving him to buy supplies; and occasionally providing brownies and iced tea with lemonade. Silent observation is very encouraging and entertaining. It was interesting and fun to watch a group of tweens in action on a project that tested their ability.

Lessons learned from Ian and crew

That group of young people working on the skateboard ramp taught me many things, including the following.

1. The power of self-confidence. Ian took a risk by initiating the project.
2. The power of leadership. Ian followed the Tom Sawyer model. He made his friends want to be involved.
3. The importance of backup. Ian had me, Bob and Tom Teller available for assistance.
4. Encouragement can take the form of watching, doing and saying nothing and not speaking doubts aloud.

5. Self-discipline – the ability to keep going no matter what– is essential. Doing chores develops this.
6. *Rule number 6*. When the hour is late and a difficult problem arises, quit and go swimming. I observed this unwritten rule in action many times. It was always a good decision. Problems look more manageable the next morning, when you're fresh. I still rely on Rule Number 6.

Chasing the Holy Grail of self-esteem

Tackling the skateboard ramp required self-esteem and commitment. Self-esteem cannot be bought at K-Mart or prescribed by a drug. Self-esteem must be nurtured in installments, like paying off a mortgage. At the beginning, paying off the loan seems impossible: it's a distant dream that requires steady payments. The only way to chip away at it is to come up with the cash one month at a time, believe in the end result, and never quit, even on the days when you have to sacrifice something else to make the payment.

In the beginning, the payments are 100 percent interest. You're giving everything and getting back only hope.

Eventually, the loan takes on a life of its own, and the amount of principle paid overtakes the amount of interest paid. It's very exciting when the loan nears maturity. Years of payments will provide a lifetime of enjoyment and housing. The sacrifices pay off. The payments become habit and feel smaller because your income and capacity have risen over the years.

Nurturing self-esteem in children is like that. **Parents must commit to regular payments.** At the beginning, the payments feel huge and the payoff is only a dream. They must build capacity gradually. Ultimately, you have nurtured a resilient capable person.

Nurturing self-esteem in children has become the Holy Grail of childhood. Because it is so essential, parents, teachers and society have gone to extremes to inject self-esteem in children. The extreme measures have resulted in what I call *self-excess-teem:* a bloated sense of self built on a shaky foundation of praise and little effort from youngsters.

Much conflicting research exists on how to unlock the Holy Grail of self-esteem. More than 10,000 studies have been conducted to de-codify it. In 1990, some 4,000 scholarly articles were written about self-esteem, more than triple the number of articles written on it in 1970, according to David P. Myers, a psychologist and author.

So important is a positive sense of self that our culture smothers children with insincere, false and underserved praise, resulting in self-excess-teem.

The danger of self-excess-teem

"Your finger painting is beautiful!" "I'm so proud of you for getting all A's on your first-grade report card!" "You played *Twinkle Twinkle Little Star* on the violin like Itzhak Perlman!"

This sugar-sweetened aggrandizement has become habitual for parents and children, in the mistaken belief that it will generate self-esteem.

Ironically, praise can contribute to self-excess-teem. When fed a junk-food diet of exaggerated praise, children can become a "praise junkie" and dependent on what others think. They may realize the content is empty, or worse, start to believe they are great and wonderful, no matter what they do. This is the irony and reality of self-excess-teem, a contagious disease among the Millennials.

Author and psychologist Jean M. Twenge describes young Americans born in the 1970s, 1980s, and 1990s as miserable, despite their entitlement and assertiveness.

From before they could talk, parents and teachers brainwashed Generation Me to believe "I am special." Parents forgot to mention that life isn't fair and effort, skill and sacrifice are required, according to Twenge.

Dubbed "Generation Me" by Twenge and also known as Gen X, Gen Y, Millennials, iGeneration, iGen and Entitlement Generation, they were raised with non-stop praise, unrealistic expectations and a low work ethic. They are ill-prepared to compete in the worst economy since the Great Depression.

GenMe has suffered ill health from a steady diet of self-excess-teem and sugared screen time. Their parents can't bear to see them suffer, be treated unfairly or fail because of the erroneous belief that it might harm their self-esteem.

Her best college students did chores

As a college writing instructor I teach all kinds of students. Some are motivated to research assignments and meet deadlines. Others seem to never hear the assignments correctly, remember the due dates, or believe that their best effort is required.

I wondered why some lack discipline and others did not, so I asked a few of my best students if they did household chores while growing up.

Jessica Humphrey said her parents encouraged her to take out the garbage, empty the dishwasher, wash the dishes, and clean her room from about the age of 10. "I never was forced to do chores in order to get a reward/present or the ability to go out with friends."

"My mom used to make drying and putting away the dishes fun by having that be our mother/daughter time. It was the one time of the day that was guaranteed to me and my mom having time to talk," Jessica said.

Jessica never got an allowance. "My parents always told me that it was a family responsibility and not a way to make money. When I was younger, I used to give my parents a hard time for not giving me money for doing chores because other kids were getting paid by their parents, but my parents were always quick to say that those kids weren't learning how a family works as a unit."

David Zangaro said his parents encouraged him to do chores and kept track using a chart they kept in the dining room. "Chores taught me time-management skills at a young age. I had to learn to balance school work, chores and play time all at once," he said.

Stephen Domzalski said by age 10 he was responsible for dusting, taking the trash/bottles out and cleaning the dishes and kitchen table after dinner. Chores helped him become responsible. "Being able to help my parents made me feel good that I was able to contribute to the household," he said.

Brian Tyburski he pitched in to help his family. "I did chores without an allowance. It was looked down (upon) if I didn't help around the house and it helped be more responsible and organized today," he said.

These were some of the best students I had had. As for the other not-so-great students? None of them even returned my calls.

Lisa Samalonis   Blackwood, New Jersey
www.singleparentsavings.wordpress.com

Ironically, suffering, finding out life *isn't* fair and failure, are powerful motivators, and even self-esteem builders.

In the workforce, GenMe must awaken to the reality that they are not wonderful no matter what; and that fulfilling their dreams will require paying dues and sacrifice. They discover there is no magic wand to make lots of money fast, with little effort.

Employers complain that young employees expect too much too soon and have high expectations for salary and promotions. Millennials demand teachers and coaches deliver high praise and high grades for low effort.

It seems improbable that failure and suffering could build self-esteem and praise erodes it. But it's true. Encouragement builds character, reliance and the self-belief of *I'm good enough to handle that.*

Chores: the anti-entitlement drug

GenMe may also face challenges in sustaining long-term relationships. In order to create a "we," each partner must sacrifice some "I" to create a sustainable "we."

Young people raised with every desire fulfilled and praised for alleged perfection may have a hard time honoring a long-term, commitment to what is sure to be an imperfect marriage.

The four cornerstones of marriage are: compromise, sacrifice, generosity and forgiveness, the most important of which is compromise.

Young people who have life customized for their convenience may be surprised when they discover the fuel to sustain a marriage is to consider how your actions/desires/words impact your partner.

This contradicts what they've been taught: to *receive* and not to *give* to others, with no immediate self-gratification.

Who would want to marry or hire a self-centered person?

This is a reminder of why using money to manipulate children is a bad idea, and why children benefit from contributing to the common good, without pay.

Entitlement develops when parents, childcare providers, teachers and coaches constantly serve children, and they are not required to give anything back, unless there's something in it for them.

Stalwartness on the job

My husband Bob owns and operates Red Oak Renovations, which specializes in remodeling kitchens and bathrooms. One day a friend called and said, "Bob, would you hire my nephew Jeffrey? He's been having a hard time. He went to college for a few semesters, is living at home and needs a job."

Bob agreed to give Jeffrey a chance.

Jeffrey had received every advantage in life. He grew up in an affluent suburb and graduated from a high school with an excellent reputation. At college, Jeffrey eschewed studying for partying, dropped out and moved into his parents' basement. Jeffrey had trouble finding and keeping a job.

Jeffrey's father drove Jeffrey to work because his driver's license had been suspended for drunk driving. His mother made lunch for him daily.

"His mother making his lunch said a lot about who he was," Bob said.

On the sixth day of work, Jeffrey called in sick. "I guessed he was hungover," Bob said. During his three weeks on Red Oak's payroll, Jeffrey frequently arrived late and sometimes with alcohol on his breath.

When Jeffrey showed up to work, he criticized all of his efforts and expected perfection, even though he was the least skilled apprentice on the crew.

Jeffrey took little initiative on the job site and watched the clock eagerly for a smoke break. He couldn't hide his entitlement, self-excess-teem and lack of self-awareness.

Bob despises firing people, but Jeffrey made it easy because he lacked the ability to show up regularly with a good attitude and learn new skills on the job.

Jeffrey's self-excess-teem ran deep. A year after Bob fired him, I answered the company phone.

"Is Bob there?" If Jeffrey had paid attention, he would have saved Bob's cell phone number, the surest way to reach him during the day.

"Who's calling?" I said.

"Jeffrey. I used to work for Bob. I wanted to know if he needed help."

I didn't recognize his voice. I said, "What kind of work did you do?"

"Oh, everything. Carpentry, tiling, painting, flooring, putting in windows. Stuff like that."

My brain made the connection. On the line was one of Bob's least-favorite ex- workers, full of self-excess-teem.

"I'll tell Bob you called." Jeffrey sounded hopeful and expectant that he deserved to be hired again.

That night, I told Bob about the call. "Will you give him another chance?"

Bob shook his head. "You don't always get a second chance in life."

I include this story about a young adult and stories about teenagers to emphasize that teenagers are made, not born, from age 2 to 12.

Jeffrey had learned what his parents had taught during the formative years: to be waited on; expect pay and praise for his efforts, no matter how paltry; and to be protected from the consequences of decisions.

The natural consequence of a crashed car

If one of my teenagers ever had their license suspended for drunk driving, they would experience the natural consequence and bike to work, take public transit or get a ride from a co-worker. They would have to make their own lunches, pay rent and attend a program to address their drinking.

All of these measures would earn back their self-respect.

We would not feel sorry for them. I would hope they would learn from the experience. I would never say this aloud.

In the August before her first year of college, Kristen accidentally totaled the "teen beater" car she shared with Ian.

We did not replace it immediately because they were headed back to college where no car was needed.

For the last three weeks of August, Kristen needed to get to work ten miles away at a coffeehouse. She got up at 5 am to bike there and asked co-workers for rides home or partway home. I gave her a few rides when it was convenient.

If it doesn't kill you, it makes you stronger. Biking to work made her stronger.

An ideal worker is made, not born

Bob replaced Jeffrey with Derek Devenne, another friend-of-a-friend. Derek worked for Bob for two years, starting at age 18. Derek showed up on time, almost never called in sick, followed directions, had reasonable expectations, proved to be a fast learner; and had a good sense of humor.

"Derek was an ideal employee. I could count on him. I hated to see him go," said Bob. Derek had commuted thirty-five miles a day to work with Bob.

After Derek started a new job, he sent Bob this email.

"I just checked out the new website. I was looking at the pictures, and they brought back a lot of great memories. I'll never forget who taught me most of the things I know now about construction and made it a job that I actually wanted to go to every day."

The work ethics of Derek and Jeffrey couldn't have been more opposite. Derek did not suffer from self-excess-teem. He came to work on time with adequate self-esteem to learn new skills and follow directions.

This is how Derek described his childhood:

I started helping out around the house by age 6, helping my dad rake the leaves with my baby rake and shoveling snow in the driveway. I was always looking for something to do outside. I constantly helped my dad with fix-up jobs, like repairing the porch, painting rooms, putting up pictures and shelves.

My parents bought me a fake plastic tool set, but I wasn't having that. I wanted to use the real tools and fix anything I could. I took things apart just for fun, like flashlights, my bike, toys, trucks, and anything that could be taken apart. Sometimes they wouldn't get back together because I had forgotten how to re-assemble them.

I started mowing the lawn at age 9. I looked for things to do with my hands. When my father got out a tool to work on something, I was right by his side, trying to help out. On Christmas, I spent the day assembling mine and my sister's toys.

My set chores were to clean up my room and the play area. I usually helped my mom to clean when she asked me. As I got older, I helped my dad more and more, instead of just watching and handing him tools. Helping my dad with the jobs he did around the house helped me to be a hard worker.

Working with tools wasn't a job for me -- it was what I did for fun. The many years working with my father were a big help when I started working for Bob in 2006, when I was 18, because I enjoy working and remodeling houses.

The right amount of self-esteem

Like every asset – emotional, physical and material – too much self-esteem is a curse. Think of *Goldilocks and the Three Bears:* The humble heroine seeks balance – porridge that's not too hot or cold, a chair that's not too big or too small, and a bed that's not too soft or hard. She wants it "just right."

Like Goldilocks, humans need just enough self-esteem.

Without sufficient self-esteem, children start the race in the back of the pack. With self-excess-teem, children can become egocentric, narcissistic and lonely in their self-aggrandized world.

Authentic self-esteem is not comparative or competitive. Nathaniel Brandon, author of seven books on self-esteem, states that genuine self-esteem reflects an attitude of "I'm okay just the way I am."

When describing twenty-four ways children develop self-esteem, Brandon concurs with multiple experts: **Children who are accepted by parents without constantly having to perform and demonstrate their merits,** have a huge advantage to develop solid self-esteem.

Ironically, praise-ful parents undermine their efforts because they create a praise junkie, oriented to make others happy and look good. Through research and experience with clients, Brandon summarized the two tenets to nurturing healthy self-esteem in children as follows.

1. Children feel accepted as "good enough" in the eyes of their parents.

2. Children feel visible to their parents. Children instinctively want approval from parents. They ache for parents to witness them.

High self-esteem is no guarantee

Positive self-esteem is no panacea. Healthy self-esteem will not prevent drug use, teenage pregnancy or delinquency, according researchers Wesley R. Burr, and Clark Christensen.

Even though self-esteem is an elusive enigma, it's better to have it than not. Cultivating the right amount of self-esteem is like trying too hard to fall asleep: the harder you try to fall asleep, the more likely you will stay awake.

Feeding children false praise, awarding meaningless trophies for low-grade participation and giving unearned high grades generates self-excess-teem and entitlement.

Too much and too little self-esteem can be problematic and leave the child vulnerable to unfavorable outside influences.

Chores plant seeds of entrepreneurship

In the mid-1970s, Saturday morning was the time to do our chores: cleaning the bathroom, dusting, vacuuming, cleaning my room, grooming the dog and doing the dishes – which I don't like to do to this day.

The best job was dusting. At the time, there wasn't much on television for kids– except for Saturday morning cartoons. If I got the job of dusting, I could be in the living room and watch cartoons at the same time.

From an early time in my life, doing chores instilled in me the concept that everyone helped to keep up the house.

At age 13, my parents divorced and my mother said, "If you want the nice jeans and what everyone else has, you need to get a job." I did. At 13, I had a temporary summer job and at 14, a regular part-time job. I've been working pretty much ever since.

Teajai Kimsey   Wichita, Kansas
Internet marketing strategist--www.IdeasThatWork.net

The power of giving children adult tasks

With nine children, my mother couldn't do everything when we were growing up. She always had a housekeeper, especially when she worked outside of the home. We didn't have to clean, but we did dishes together every night.

Some tasks had more status than others, like being in charge of washing the pots and pans. Only older children could be the washer because of the skill required. My mother complained vociferously if a still-dirty pot was put away in the cupboard. She had standards we were expected to meet.

At about 12 years old, my mother gave us permission to sit at her desk to write out the monthly bills. It was a highly-prized job because of the skill required and the trust it implied. We helped her and learned how to pay bills and practice generosity.

Numerous charities solicited my parents for donations. She placed the requests in a stack with the instruction to write $5 checks to each of them. In the 1970s, $5 was equal to $25 in today's dollars, no paltry amount for the mother of nine to give away.

The value of donating money has stayed with me as well as the pride I felt in writing out the checks for her signature, preparing the envelopes and mailing them.

Practice moderation in chores

Doing a reasonable number of adult tasks gives a young person a feeling they belong, that their contribution makes a difference.

A 27-year-old woman wrote in my survey, "I learned to wield a hatchet by age 9 and an axe by 12. I was expected to cut and stack firewood daily after school" for her working-class family. One of her parents had died and she had to contribute around the house to the point where she sometimes resented it.

She agreed with these statements about chores: "Taught me responsibility, instilled a work ethic in me, motivated me to have my own children do chores now or in the future, made me resentful THEN and NOW I see the value."

The act of chopping wood daily requires self-discipline and competence. It's interesting the 27-year-old woodchopper also said she intends have her own children do chores.

Ideally, parents practice moderation in the quantity of chores children do to avoid resentment and provide a normal childhood.

Almost none of the respondents younger than age 30 complained they had to do too many chores while growing up. Complaints about being over-burdened came from those born before 1964.

Children will rise to our expectations, even stretch to meet them, as did the woodchopper.

A 57-year old man said he "sometimes did the grocery shopping at age 7 and cared for the family boat in Florida starting at age 10." He agreed that chores taught him responsibility and doing them was an advantage in life. He said, "I had fewer chores than my sisters, which always seemed weird to me and made me feel bad."

I'm sure he never asked his parents to give him more chores.

Chores generate responsibility and self-esteem

Through chores, children can develop a positive self-concept anchored in reality and connect to their family.

My survey found no relationship between doing chores and positive self-esteem. However, more than three-fourths of the people who had regular chores while growing up said it developed responsibility in them. When youngsters are held accountable to perform simple jobs around the house for others, without compensation, they are depended upon by others and connected to their family. **Chores create a platform upon which to nurture self-worth.**

The chore can be as simple as a toddler using a plastic rake to build a tiny pile of leaves beside her father or a sullen teenager quickly making huge sloppy piles of leaves in the dusk alone on a Friday night after procrastinating all week so she can go out Friday night.

Raking done by any age child creates the same internal message: "I'm important and connected to my family. I'm seen. What I do for them matters. I make a difference to them."

Performing age-appropriate chores for the common good at home without bribery, threats or punishment teaches responsibility and establishes selflessness and self-confidence.

Chores and encouragement teach children to work hard for what they want. If they fail or don't get what they want the first time, they have the courage and confidence to try again. Children learn to do chores for the sake of the chore and whether they feel like it or not. This counteracts entitlement because children learn they have to produce, not just consume and perform to make parents look good.

New practice: At the next family meeting, encourage children to take responsibility for an adult task. Let them suggest one, and support them to do it for a week, even if it's a stretch.

Challenge: Break the habit of lavishing praise or offering constant criticism. Trust your children can handle the outcome of their decisions.

For group discussion or journaling: Describe memories when you felt either empowered or deeply discouraged because of something your parents said or did. How has that impacted your parenting style?

Key points from Self-Excess-Teem

- Nurture self-esteem by making steady deposits of encouragement.
- Hold high expectations for youngsters to contribute to household work.
- Lavishing praise may create self-excess-teem, which may be as problematic as low-self-esteem.
- When a youngster takes on an ambitious project, offer support and encouragement, and stay out of his way.
- Nurture self-esteem by accepting children as "good enough," and ensure children feel seen and witnessed.
- There is no magic pill to capture the Holy Grail of self-esteem.
- Lay the foundation for self-esteem and self-discipline in the first dozen years.

Do what you love and never go to work a day in your life.
Confucius

13
Wax on, Wax off
The Zen of Work

In "The Karate Kid" (Columbia Pictures 1984) a teenage boy experiences how a strict mentor and manual labor can be profound teachers.

The karate kid, Daniel LaRusso (played by Ralph Macchio), moves with his mother from New Jersey to the San Fernando Valley of California after his father's death.

A victim of bullies at his new high school, Daniel connects with the eccentric handyman of his building, Mr. Miyagi (played by Pat Morita), a war veteran and karate master. Daniel wants to learn karate to defend against the bullies.

The two make a deal. Mr. Miyagi says: "I promise to teach karate. You promise to learn. What I say, you do, no question." Daniel agrees.

Mr. Miyagi put Daniel to work washing and waxing several classic cars. "Wax on, right hand. Wax off, left hand. Breathe in through the nose, out through the mouth. Wax on, wax off. Remember to breathe. It's very important," Miyagi said, ignoring Daniel's protests.

"You promise to do what I say, no question," Miyagi said, and left Daniel to do the chore, which he completed exhausted, by moonlight.

Miyagi and Daniel repeated the scenario three more times. Daniel sanded a huge outdoor deck with the motion, "right circle, left circle, breathe in, breathe out." He painted the boards of a long tall fence right-handed, and the small boards left-handed, up and down. He painted the house with brush strokes from left to right. Daniel accompanied every motion with synchronistic breathing, per Miyagi's instructions.

Exasperated and fatigued, Daniel was ready to quit until Miyagi showed him how the repetitious work unconsciously taught Daniel karate moves. The movie ended when Daniel triumphed over the bullies in a karate tournament. Daniel got the girl, too.

The fable dramatizes how work relates to personal power and achievement. **It also illustrates how youngsters need encouragement to do chores so that they can embrace the Zen of Work.**

Work with joy

As the child of teachers who had a low income and high ideals in Virginia, I had to help out and I loved it. When I was 5 years old, I contributed ideas to the house we built. At 7, I helped to sand wood for the living room walls. At 10, I poured concrete for the back porch.

All that gave me a lesson in planning and follow-through.

By the time I was 8, I was cooking and learning to sew. Every spring, the three of us kids pitched in to prepare and tend the garden. By 10, I was helping to can tomatoes and make jam. By 13, I was helping to run the house because my mother had died in 1956.

All this was a gift: skills, resilience and all the stories I learned as we worked. My parents demonstrated meaningful and satisfying work. They taught us to be resourceful and creative.

It's not surprising that my career today is to help people to work with integrity, purpose and joy.

Pat McHenry Sullivan   Oakland, California
www.spiritworkandmoney.com

A warning to parents: the movie was a dramatization. Hope for but don't expect a similar transformation with children and chores. You may encounter resistance, protest and avoidance. Be pleased when they complete the chore in a reasonable time. Remain caring, firm, and

Express passion through work

An internationally recognized artist for drawings, paintings and sculptures of dancers, Pablo Solomon traces his success back to a work ethic that was instilled during childhood, in a poor neighborhood in Houston, where he was born in 1947.

My father worked all his life, mainly for the railroad. My mother grew up as a sharecropper. We never went without a meal, but money was never in abundance.

I worked from childhood cutting lawns, delivering circulars, cleaning boats, and working in restaurants of family members. By the time I was 10 years old, I had my own bank account and was expected to use my own money for anything other than necessities.

I was recognized as having ability in art at a young age and began selling my art by my teenage years. I worked my way through college with scholarships, by loading trucks, in the oilfields, repairing diesel locomotives, for an auction, and as a restaurant cook.

Having worked from a young age has taught me to be disciplined and to value work. I still get up every day at 4 a.m. to begin my day as an artist.

Parents do their children a disservice by not requiring them to work and to contribute. Too many young people today not only do not value work, but do not make the connection between hard work and success.

Finding work that one enjoys is one of the major factors in having a happy and successful life. I am thankful that my love for art eventually gave me a way to make a living.

Pablo Solomon   Lampasas, Texas
Artist and designer--www.pablosolomon.com

demanding. Don't be sidetracked or beaten down by incessant negotiations, all of which must be acceptable to you. Hold a vision and be committed to youngsters contributing around the house. Like many challenges of parenting, anticipate a delayed payoff.

"The Karate Kid" shows that menial work can be a powerful teacher. Work demands mindfulness. **Be with the work, whatever it is, and the work will provide its own reward.**

Love the work you're with

A visit to a café in the swank South End of Boston on a Friday night reminded me of the importance of being with your work, whatever it is.

A good-looking 20-something waiter greeted our party of four: Bob, me, Casey and her boyfriend Terrence. We were willing to share our jovial mood with the server.

"How are you tonight?" the server said with some sincerity when he greeted us.

"Fine. How are you?" I said.

"Okay, except for this thing called 'work,'" the server said just under his breath. He paused, and said a little louder, "What can I get you to drink?"

The server went to fetch the drinks.

"I guess he's not too happy to come to work," I said.

"Ma, most people do not love their jobs," Casey said.

"Then they should find one they love, or at least love the one they're with," I said.

"That's impossible," Casey said, exasperated that I didn't understand her point of view.

"Either change the situation or change your attitude towards the situation," I said. Work is a major part of life. Even retired and independently wealthy people find a meaningful way to use their days.

The young waiter had followed his whim all day, and then came to work just for the money, one of the worst motivations for working. He missed being in the present moment with us and clouded ours. We left a minimum tip.

Dirty diapers in every job

From age 22 to 31, I had a *wax on, wax off* experience of eleven consecutive years of babies in diapers. My mother liked to remind me, "Every job has dirty diapers."

Mildred was right. Every job has stinky mundane aspects. "Dirty diapers" is an apt euphemism. As a domo-guru, dirty diapers weren't that bad. Diaper-changing was an opportunity to stop keeping house and pay attention to my baby. To nuzzle her soft tummy, sing a little rhyme, to connect with her after she had done her jobs of sleeping, eliminating, and playing alone or watching her siblings. Changing her diaper gave me a moment with a tiny bit of perfection.

Contrast that with Pam, who struggled to pin down her babies to change their diapers. Her two toddlers knew Pam considered changing diapers disdainful. Their wrestling matches and resistance reflected her joyless attitude towards spending a few minutes caring for their well-being. It's all in our attitude, and infants-to-teens are expert interpreters of parents' non-verbal language.

The emptiness of working for money

Our culture's attitude towards work has shifted from being a way to contribute to society and find meaning in life, to being a way to generate wealth, and to heartlessly leverage others in that quest.

Beware. Working just for the money is a bankrupt quest. Dr. Larry Linden, career counselor and author said, "Taking a job just for the money is a bad idea. I can almost guarantee it won't work out."

"Work" has three ladder rungs. On the first rung, a person can perfunctorily perform a job for a paycheck. On the next rung, a person can have a career, which requires training, specialized knowledge and a reputation. The person can enjoy the career, its achievements, contributions and peer recognition, but at the end of the day, it's still just a job. They'd rather be doing something else.

The highest rung of the career ladder is when a person's passion is their life work, a reflection of their essence. They love their work and look forward to it. It is a joy to go to work.

Our society has lost reverence for work and reduced it to earning income, as much as possible, as easily as possible. Manual labor and traditional women's work has lost status.

Laurie Gray, a lawyer with one child, has a typical attitude towards housework. "I cook and clean and do laundry because it needs to be done. I'd still much rather spend my time working as an attorney, or reading and writing, spending time with friends and family, or doing anything I enjoy," Gray said.

Her attitude is typical and reasonable, given the extraordinary demands on women employed full-time while raising children. Their time is in a

Dogs are friends and teachers

I wanted a dog, and my father said, "Fine, but you have to train the dog, and take care of it, or no dog." When I was 9 years old, we got Queenie, a German Shepherd.

My father showed me how to train the dog on a leash, and to heel, sit and stay. I was responsible for the training lessons, which I did in a gentle manner until Queenie learned the commands.

My parents and I took turns feeding and grooming her. I learned responsibility and how to understand and communicate with Queenie. We both loved to play hide and seek. Queenie gave me great joy, wonder and a sense of pride.

Queenie was smart and may have saved my baby brother's life. While playing on the front lawn, my brother followed a rolling ball into the street. I tried to catch him as he chased the ball, which was headed into the path of an oncoming car. Queenie was faster. She ran over, grabbed his diaper between her teeth, and pulled him back onto the grass just as the car passed the house. My brother started crying. She licked him until he hugged her.

I would have never reached my brother in time to prevent a tragedy. I often think about what might have happened if Queenie had not rescued him.

Diane T. Creston   New York, New York
President/creative director--www.crestonadvertising.com

vice, held tight on both ends by children, spouse, work and their own needs.

Many Westerners aspire to join a wealthy class that's removed from doing the mundane tasks of daily life. The more money we have, the more services we can buy to avoid cleaning, yard work, cooking, child care, home maintenance, sewing and more. Instead of using a shovel or rake, we hire someone and drive to the gym for a workout.

After avoiding the work of life, people feel disconnected and depressed. A psychologist listens to them and possibly prescribes medication.

The "serve me" attitude trickles over to leisure time where we hire people to entertain us at clubs, theaters, on vacation and in classes. Disney World, Club Med and other resorts offer total-care vacations that require little effort other than the price of admission. **We have forgotten the joy of creating our own fun.**

Napkin and salad girl starts a tradition

As the youngest in my family, I wasn't big enough to help my sisters, nine and twelve years older, to cook dinner.

When I was 4, my parents gave me the job of setting the table and title of Napkin Girl. I carefully folded the paper napkins and put a knife and a spoon on the right. I set two forks, one for the main course and one for the salad, on the napkin.

When I was older, I was in charge of making the salad. I could put anything in, chopped the way I wanted. I proudly served the salad in a big wooden bowl and knew everyone would love it. Of all my household chores, I loved best being Napkin Girl and Salad Girl.

Setting the table showed me the value of taking the time and care to create a beautiful table, which makes a meal special. When I was allowed to make the salad any way I wanted, it showed me I could be creative and that people would enjoy my creativity. Today, I'm known among my friends for giving a great dinner party and for my outstanding and unusual salads.

Patti Ann Wood   Decatur, Georgia
Body language expert--www.pattiwood.net

Work, in the home and at a job, is seen as something to get done, instead of something to contribute to the world and your family.

When I asked a 24-year-old man, "What do you want to do with your life?" he said, "I want to make money and be financially free by the time I'm 35," he said. His answer is typical of the Millennials. The trouble is that many youths are ignorant of the steps in between.

Full-time employment takes the majority of a typical person's time. It's practical to use income to create more leisure time by hiring people to do some cleaning, cooking, childcare and yard work. To structure one's life to escape manual labor denies us the experience of creating something from scratch, connecting to our home and the earth.

I love to pull dandelions from the yard one at a time by hand. It feels good and makes my yard look good. I avoid applying harsh herbicides that would run off into the adjacent pond. Pulling dandelions is dirty. I get blisters and a backache. I'll never beat the dandelions. Their seeds are too abundant. Even though I lose the war against them, I get lost in the battle and forget everything else. I feel good. That is the Zen of Work.

Cleaning as a ritual

When we sold the house where we raised our children for sixteen years, I took time off my day job and spent two days cleaning it, allegedly for the new owners.

My unconscious purpose was to go through each room carefully and lovingly, in a "good-bye" to a cherished place. Every room held a spectrum of memory and feeling. I closed the door on my time as a domo-guru, to my children's youth, and many transitions of life and marriage. Scrubbing, mopping, vacuuming, sweeping and dusting every room played out as a requiem to reflect on the rhapsody in the place.

In my new home, finding out where the cobwebs grow has been a way to make it my home. For the first two years I lived here I was employed full-time at a job with a forty-minute commute. To save $2,700 a year on house cleaners and put it towards college tuition, Bob and I periodically geared up to "power clean" the house on a Saturday morning.

Bob's attitude toward cleaning is like flushing a toilet: do it quickly because it stinks and you must; take advantage of technology and chemicals; don't look too closely; and get away fast.

Cleaning the house paid us each about $50 an hour. We cleaned fast to get to leisure activities, but I found little satisfaction in power cleaning. It reduced cleaning to an unpleasant task and stole the Zen out of beautifying my home.

Now that I work from home, I have the luxury to spend ten or fifteen minutes a day in cleaning something really well. I stop thinking and fall into the Zen of caring for my home.

Physical work feels good

It's snowing heavily as I write these words. I just shoveled snow off the roof to prevent ice dams. I like the resounding *thump* of snow falling from the roof. Balancing on the roof made me focus on the task. It felt good to protect my house from ice dams and a possible roof collapse, and to give Bob one less thing to do. Plus, I love snow.

Some people would view shoveling the snow from the roof as an onerous task; however, it's all in the attitude. It gave me a break, got my heart rate up and filled my lungs with clean cold air. It cleared my mind and inspired this chapter.

Mowing the lawn can have the same Zen. Pushing the mower around the yard in neat rows, the odor of freshly cut grass and inspecting the yard serves double-duty as yard work and a workout.

For Judy, a single mother of four teens, yard work creates solitary time. "When I mow the lawn, nobody bothers me then. I enjoy it," she said.

After dinner or a party at a friend's house, I gravitate towards the sink to wash dishes. I feel rejected when the hostess says, "Leave it, Susan, we'll do it later," and pushes me to the parlor. They don't realize I associate dishes with the camaraderie I had with my siblings while doing dishes.

Be present with the dishes, soap and water

Thich Nhat Hanh uses dishes and everything in his life to practice being in the present moment. He finds joy in being with the hot water, soap and dishes.

The Zen Buddhist monk takes time to see the dirt on each dish. He is in no hurry to eat dessert sooner by rushing through the dishes. Rushing through doing the dishes would diminish the quality of that moment.

His goal is to be fully present in each moment. Hanh views his hands, the dishes themselves, and the time to do the dishes as miracles. He says if he does dishes without joy, it will be impossible for him to find joy in eating dessert. If he is constantly fixated on the next moment, he misses the present moment: the flavor, smell and texture of dessert, the effort of the cooks, the wonderful sensation of eating it.

By constantly hurrying and thinking ahead, the present moment is lost, according to Hanh. He prefers to go slower and take extra time on the dishes. **It is the practice of living fully in the present moment while doing something necessary.**

The Zen of working together in a community

After dinner or an event at our Unitarian church, people in our community immediately start putting away chairs, folding up tables and washing dishes. We care about our meetinghouse and work together to put everything away so the space is ready for the next gathering.

I cherish the time with my community, before, during and after an event. We take turns taking care of each other, in different ways, like a family.

Do for others

Work to benefit others can be transformative.

One day, I came home from my reporter's job feeling enraged at my editor. I stomped out to the mailbox and decided to make a pot of carrot soup.

I vigorously chopped carrots, celery, potatoes and onions. In the midst of the slicing and dicing, I thought, *Bob will like this soup. I will enjoy this soup.* My frown and my heart lifted slightly.

I stirred in the broth and flavorings, tasted it and thought, *This soup is delicious. I'm going to make people happy with this soup.* The noose of anger loosened its grip. The chopping, stirring and anticipation of joy I would bring to others dissolved the anger at my boss.

The modern perception of work

Manual labor got a bad rap in the twentieth century when Americans left the farm and joined a consumer society. People abandoned the agrarian lifestyle, unpleasant odors, hard work, unpredictable weather and sometimes poverty. Factory farming freed people from the toil of farming.

Then, the average farmer fed six people from one acre. Today, large-scale mechanized farming can feed 126 people per acre. Compare that to an organic farm, such as Red Fire Farm in Granby, Mass., which supplies vegetables to about seventy-six people per acre.

With higher yields per acre, poor and working class people can afford to leave the farm behind, keep their hands clean and embrace manufactured goods and food.

In the 1950s and 1960s, TV shows such as "Hee Haw," "Green Acres," and "Mayberry RFD" reflected America's cultural shift away from farm life and branded farmers as backward, simple and even stupid.

On the contrary, farming is not for stupid people. A farmer must be a Renaissance man or woman. A farmer knows how to fix a tractor, birth a calf and when and where to plant seeds. Farmers wrestle with unpredictable weather, manage a small business, and partner with the mystery of seeds, and plant and animals reproduction.

The Millennial Generation has made an unexpected detour back to the land, with a new model of community supported, small-scale organic farming. They are embracing the rural life their grandparents and parents eschewed. Young people have started a movement to return to the land and work on organic farms, live in community and sometimes give up eating meat.

The new wave of organic farmers hardly resembles the hayseeds on "Hee Haw." It is dirty hard work at the whim of the weather.

Computers aren't the answer

At the other end of the spectrum, many young people deign manual labor.

"I want to have a job where I don't have to wash my hands before dinner," said a young man in a radio interview. He was the son of a first-generation immigrant who embraced American ideals: work in an office, keep your hands clean. Let someone else do the dirty work.

181

We humans instinctively seek higher status and the easiest path. With the shift to a consumer economy, many people can't or don't fix and maintain homes and machines. Instead of changing the oil or raking leaves with youngsters on a Saturday afternoon, we hire others to do it. Father and son can be found inside playing simulated golf in front of a jumbo TV screen. At least they're spending time together, but they're missing an opportunity to work on a real project.

We glorify computer work and play as the pinnacles of achievement. Computers are clean, high-status tools and toys. They make some tasks more efficient and facilitate fast communication. **Computers have become the new pinnacle of life to be pursued and valued more highly than anything else.**

In the 1990s I objected when our middle school converted the sewing lab into a computer lab. I lost the battle and didn't bother to complain when the school eliminated wood shop for computer-aided drawing.

How will children learn to sew on a button, hammer a nail, or use a sewing machine, saw or hammer? We lose capability, connection and a work consciousness by abstaining from manual labor. Working with your hands is satisfying. Work is not only about earning money.

The Waldorf School movement is an anti-technology haven where students are taught to knit, encouraged to play with blocks and not given access to computers until eighth grade.

It's up to parents to reinforce values and skills at home, on weekends, instead of going to the mall, zoning out on sugared screen time, or purchasing pre-packaged entertainment.

Avoid using chores as punishment

To cultivate the Zen of Work, **do not use work as a punishment**, unless the work was agreed upon in advance, and is related, respectful and reasonable. If work is assigned as a punishment under the mistaken belief, "You must suffer to learn," it can engender revenge, resentment and a poor work ethic. It is particularly onerous to assign work as punishment that is perceived by the youth as unfair.

Bob's family spent summers in their cottage on Keuka Lake in the Finger Lakes of Western New York. One day when he was 12, Bob canoed up an inlet of the lake, violating a boundary set by his parents. Bob's older brother reported the incident to their parents.

"As punishment, you will do the dinner dishes all summer," said his father. The punishment did not meet the test of the Three Rs. It was not related, respectful or reasonable.

Like many punishments imposed by well-meaning parents, it had a boomerang effect and planted seeds of revenge. It hurt Bob's relationship with his parents and soured his attitude towards dishes for decades.

When Bob did the dishes every night alone for two months, resentment worked its way deep into his psyche. Bob associated doing dishes as an unjust punishment imposed from a higher authority. Doing dishes had nothing to do with going too far in the canoe.

Youngsters who get punished regularly may:

1. Lose faith in adults, feel bitter and believe "I can't trust you."

2. May get even: "They are making me do something now, but I'll get them back later."

3. Learn from the punishment, withdraw, and figure out a way to beat them: "Next time I'll be sneakier and get away with it."

4. Lose self-esteem, "I'm no good."

It's ironic that we blame teenagers like Bob for having a surly attitude. It's hard to reverse the curse of negative parenting during the first dozen years and wrestle with teens under the influence of hormones.

A related consequence for Bob would have been to restrict or ban his use of all boats for a few weeks. His parents could have said, "It's hard to trust you when you don't follow our safety rules," and "There are too many other boats in the marina for you to navigate the canoe on the inlet." Bob could have negotiated new boundaries where he could go on the lake, given his maturity.

Several Baby Boomer-era respondents to my survey complained that

---

Let them get their hands dirty

Establishing a simple chore routine and a commitment to follow through, can take an investment of fifteen minutes a week. The simpler and less appealing the chores are, the better -- like taking out the garbage, cleaning a toilet, or sweeping the floor.

their parents used chores as punishment. In some cases, it made them too hard a worker. Others like Bob felt resentful about unfair punishment. Being forced to work too hard cast pallor over work that could have been done joyfully.

Encourage young people to maintain a positive attitude towards work. Avoid using work as an unrelated punishment.

Small chores yield big results

Youngsters don't need a long list of chores to benefit from doing them. Simply taking the responsibility to do dishes every night after dinner, taking out the trash, recycling, and sweeping the floor will nurture the Zen of Work.

It is worth the investment in time and attention to involve children in household tasks.

Youths who have responsibility for chores will:

- learn to appreciate the peacefulness of working alone and the group energy of working on a team;
- contribute to the family, and give back after so much has been given to them; and
- associate power, connection, contribution, skill and self-importance to their regular jobs around the house.

Get out of dishes free

To get the maximum benefit from chores, children must "own" a few chores, meaning if they don't do them, they don't get done. With that responsibility comes the occasional holiday. My children eagerly anticipated birthday holidays from doing dishes.

When growing up, my family had the same get-out-of-dishes-free birthday policy, which I looked forward to with glee. I gloated that I didn't have to work. In reality, the clamor of doing dishes with my siblings was more fun than waiting alone until the dishes were done and we could play in the backyard.

The Zen of building a chicken coop

When I decided to keep chickens, Bob agreed to build the coop with my help. I put on work clothes and thought, *It's fun to get my hands dirty. I love the feeling of power tools cutting wood, and creating something from scraps and supplies. The smell of sawdust reminds me of my dad. It's neat to see the pieces fit together.*

Bob and I worked together to frame and attach the walls to the floor. I can see why he loves construction. At the end of the day we had built something useful and concrete.

Bob procured a gallon of stain from his workshop. "This stain needs to be stirred. It has settled," Bob said.

I found a comfortable place to sit in the sun and commenced stirring the two inches of solids that had sunk to the bottom of the can. When my father took on the same task, I remember thinking, *How does he have the patience to stir for so long? It will take forever.*

I let the task absorb me and didn't rush. I had nowhere to go except that moment. I was disappointed when my ten minute stain-stirring meditation ended.

Ironically, people spend thousands of dollars taking yoga, going to therapy and learning to meditate when all they have to do is practice being present when washing dishes, stirring paint and changing diapers.

Before building the chicken coop, I had wondered where I would find time to build it. Because it was fun and I wanted the coop, the Saturday afternoon quickly dissipated. I felt good at the end of the day.

If the children were at home, we would have involved them in building the chicken coop by finding age-appropriate tasks such as painting, getting supplies, hammering nails, using power tools with supervision, with playtime in the yard in between tasks. They would have been allowed to walk off the job after a negotiated amount of time, the work ran out, or we had to take them somewhere.

Involving children is always more hectic and time-consuming *and* worth the investment. They'll eventually build skateboard ramps and bookshelves and fix your computer. Families are built on investments of time, work and fun, which reinforce the Zen of Work.

The Zen of family work

By establishing a positive approach to work from an early age, children gain a work ethic, find joy in work, learn to follow instructions, belong to a team, and contribute to the greater good.

They'll discover how to organize their time and skills to get a job done. Discovering the *wax on, wax off* of chores prepares youngsters to be good students and employees, and grounds them in a positive attitude towards work and themselves.

New practice: Explore the *wax on, wax off* aspects of simple household chores. Create time to do dishes, clean house and rake leaves with children. Allow open-ended time to be present.

Challenge: Make time to do one task or a project you would have hired someone to do. View the time as an investment in your family.

For discussion or journaling: What is my attitude towards work and menial tasks? What kinds of work do I enjoy? Describe childhood memories of working alongside of family members on projects.

Key points from The Zen of Work

- Like the *Karate Kid,* practice being present with house work. Encourage children to find the Zen of Work when cleaning toilets, taking out trash and washing dishes.
- Appreciate the dignity, pride and skill of building, sewing, designing, repairing, cleaning, maintaining and cooking.
- Set aside time for the family or a parent and child to work together and create things from raw materials.
- Do not use chores as a punishment or consequence for misbehavior unless it is related and reasonable.

We can't solve problems by using the same kind of thinking we used when we created them.
Albert Einstein

14
Green Chores

The goals of reduce-reuse-recycle-refuse-and-revise create many chores simple enough for young children to do while instilling a new way of thinking, living and using energy. Parents create a new consciousness by encouraging the family to use less energy, generate less trash and grow a few vegetables every summer.

Parents can respond when children advocate for the Earth. When we moved to a new house a few years ago, setting up a compost system was not high on my priority list. Kristen and Ian came home from college and said, "Ma, where is the compost bucket?" This demonstrates the effectiveness of expectations and encouragement. I put "Compost" on the family meeting agenda so we could figure out where to locate it outside. We had had a compost system within a few days.

They grew up sorting trash and recycling. We reduced our weekly garbage for six people to one trash can a week by thinking and sorting everything we threw out. Such a system for trash reminds us that there is no "away" when something is thrown away. There's the added benefit that recycling is an excellent chore for children.

At the new house we no longer have the luxury of curbside recycling. We take turns hauling sorted trash to a transfer and recycling station once a month. It's inconvenient, takes time, and we're willing to do it because it reinforces our values. One payoff is to explore the "Give and Get" shed where people leave and take usable household items, toys and books. I've found many treasures there, and left my fair share, too.

When nine of us spent a week at a cottage, my offspring suggested we use cloth napkins. It was a good idea until we realized it was impossible to tell who used what napkin at the previous meal. Casey suggested we sew a different button or ribbon on the corner of each napkin to identify them. We found some extra buttons at the cottage and used them. Using cloth napkins is a small step to use less energy. Cloth napkins are also sturdy and classy.

I use handkerchiefs instead of tissues, and rags instead of paper towels, as much as possible. We haven't replaced toilet paper, even though people in developing countries splash water instead of using toilet paper. All of the habits of our lifestyle add up to Westerners having five or ten times the carbon footprint of people in developing countries. With a little extra effort and a few extra chores we can steer towards lowering our carbon footprint.

Beyond convenience

Changing how we use energy requires inconvenience, attention and setting up new systems. We set up a system to dry clothes indoors near the furnace, which luckily, is adjacent to the washer and dryer. It takes a few extra minutes to hang up everything on a steel clothesline, hangars and a wooden clothes rack. It takes longer to dry, so planning is necessary. Like many aspects of sustainability, it's inconvenient.

There are payoffs. The coarse air-dried towels provide a free exfoliator, without going to a pricey spa. The towels soften up after a few uses. Hang-drying the majority of laundry reduces our electric bill by 20 to 30 percent. Among household appliances, clothes dryers are second to refrigerators for using the most energy. Hanging clothes is an excellent way for small children to work beside parents, and for children over age 11 to practice sustainability when doing their own laundry.

Hang-drying requires a paradigm shift. I don't want to hang out our "dirty laundry," *and* I love the smell and feel of sheets dried on an outdoor clothesline. Hang-drying inside is more convenient than trooping outside, especially in winter.

Reducing your carbon footprint requires inconvenience, while creating a plethora of chores for children and families. It encourages us to go back in time when people used clotheslines, rode buses, ate locally-grown food, and shared cars and rides.

Turn off one light bulb at a time

Parents have the opportunity to model a sustainable lifestyle. One evening my father came home and pulled me aside on the front lawn.

"Is that light on in your room?" Dad said, pointing to the third floor where a forty-watt incandescent light bulb had illuminated my empty bedroom all day.

"Yes," I said, wondering why a single light bulb was that important.

"Go turn it off now," he said.

Going up two flights of steps to shut off the light bulb gave my 10-year-old psyche time to internalize his value and pledge to never again to waste energy of the light bulb or my energy to climb the steps.

Like many people who came of age during the Great Depression, John embodied the lifestyle of reduce, reuse and recycle. He loved junkyards and dumpsters. John recycled building materials, tools and engines. He unscrewed bolts and reused them. He practiced the lost art of fixing things instead of throwing them out.

Our tribe knew the simple rules of the house, and many of them included energy use. Don't waste hot water by doing dishes in running water, taking deep baths or long showers. Turn off lights. Put on a sweater instead of turning up the heat. Don't waste food. Ride your bike for transportation and put it in the garage at night. Use the car only when necessary and for multiple chained errands. We were trained to conserve even in the era of twenty-nine-cents-a-gallon gasoline.

Encourage independence if possible

Minimizing car use was a family policy that provided exercise and independence. Before I could get a ride from my parents or an older sibling, I had to prove I could not walk, bike, roller skate, take the bus or carpool. I loved the freedom of my bike and riding the bus.

At 9 years old, I said to my mother, "Can I have piano lessons?" She enrolled me at the Wilmington Music School, drove me to the first lesson and said, "Next week you can walk here after school." That was the only time my mother drove me during six years of piano lessons. I perceived it took a long time to walk home from music school. It turns out that the music school was a half-mile from my elementary school and 1.2 miles from home, a half-hour walk. Not far.

No one ever tried to kidnap me. In fact, the incident of stranger danger hasn't changed much since Baby Boomers were children. It was always an adventure to walk, bike or roller skate to lessons. If I stopped at the corner store for a treat, the calories burned off without effort. Walking to piano lessons developed responsibility and confidence for how to navigate in the world.

The old-fashioned tradition of walking to school

Parents are so afraid of the slim chance of child abduction that it's rare for Millennials to go anywhere by their own foot-power. Many parents drive children to school or to the school bus stop for safety, convenience, necessity and to spend more time together.

Only 16 percent of American school children walk or bike to school, compared to 42 percent in 1969.

Walking to school is so unusual that the government sponsors a national "Walk to School Day." Parents in some communities operate "walking school buses" and take turns leading groups of children to school the old-fashioned way. Walking to school is a chore of sorts, and an opportunity for fitness and independence, while reducing energy consumption.

Ease the grip of stranger-danger

Children benefit from age-appropriate independence, according to Lenore Skenazy, author of *Free Range Kids*. Skenazy rose to fame after she gave permission for her 9-year-old son to take the subway alone in New York City. Through impeccable research, Skenazy debunks parents' worst nightmare to prove the world is as safe as or safer than 40 years ago, contrary to the media's efforts to convince us that a child molester lurks at every school bus stop. **The rates of child abduction and murder have remained steady for the past forty years.**

Strangers kidnap about 100 children annually in America. Statistically, that boils down to a one-in-1.5 million chance of really bad luck. The majority of missing children are quickly found. Except for the extremely rare case of kidnapping by a stranger, **nearly all missing youths are either runaways, or kidnapped by an estranged family member.** Children are at a much higher risk to be in an auto accident, another kind of accident, or getting cancer or the flu. It's more likely to be struck by lightning, a one-in-700,000 chance, than to be kidnapped by a stranger.

The Amber Alert and media prey on our fears and vividly dramatize predators. **This grossly exaggerated threat has changed how children navigate in the world.** Some parents drive children everywhere to avoid be judged as jeopardizing their children's health and safety, and/or to keep up with everyone else. Using less energy for transportation requires a paradigm shift about children's safety and parents' behavior.

One option is biking. I love biking for transportation and recreation and with my family. Biking can reduce a person's carbon footprint while getting exercise, spending time together and going to school and work. Bikes can to save the planet because bicycling naturally encourages people to live, work and go to school nearby. Bike commuting was once the high point of my day. Biking isn't a chore so much as it's a habit and an opportunity for parents to model sustainability, independence and fitness. In congested areas, biking is more convenient and faster than driving.

Transportation is one of the top three ways Americans use energy. Heating and lighting buildings and growing and delivering food use more energy than transportation.

Go on a Low Carbon Diet together

The Low Carbon Diet, a Thirty-Day Program to Lose 5,000 Pounds of carbon dioxide by David Gershon is a workbook to form new habits to reduce energy use. The book calls for small groups to meet four times to evaluate how they use energy, plan to make changes in their home and lifestyle, and then report and support each other in implementing the changes.

Families can take on *The Low Carbon Diet* at family meetings and invite others in the community to join the effort to reduce, reuse, recycle, refuse, and revise. The *Low Carbon Diet* covers myriad ways to change. The next step is to take it to the next level and change our industrial systems. It starts with changing your mental paradigm, followed by action: having a few family meetings and undertaking projects to set up new home systems to use less energy.

Cultivate a few tomatoes and chickens

Growing a few vegetable plants is a simple, effective and satisfying way for families to move towards living and eating more locally. Children can perform the chores of cultivating and harvesting vegetables. Even apartment dwellers can plant a few cucumber seeds in a five-gallon pail. Ambitious urban gardeners can share space at a community garden. Growing a few cucumbers or tomatoes organically teaches children the connection between earth and food, with the bonus of producing something delicious, fresh and fun, even if it's a small something. Children can enjoy growing their own plants and flowers.

If you have the capability and ambition, raising chickens brings a miniature web of life among animals, people, food and recycling into your own backyard. Very young children can help care for the chickens. School-age children can raise their own chickens. Building a chicken coop is an ideal project for a carpenter as young as 12 or 13, and as a family project.

Backyard chickens have many built-in chores, including opening and closing the henhouse in the morning and at night, collecting eggs, cleaning the coop, and delivering water and kitchen scraps to the birds. Chickens are omnivores and will consume most leftovers. Chicken manure provides local fertilizer. The rewards include the antics of the birds, the thrill of a warm, just-hatched egg, and the taste. The taste of eggs raised in my backyard is beyond compare.

Novices can gain knowledge and share the care and feeding of chickens by forming a neighborhood egg cooperative. After a year or two of experience in a cooperative, it's less daunting to set up a backyard coop with six chickens. Chickens can be raised for meat. It's easy to learn how to butcher chickens and do it together. Raising backyard chickens is a fun family project to share.

A significant way to lower your carbon footprint is to eat less meat and dairy products. Put "Meatless Meals on Monday" on the next family meeting agenda and discuss suggestions to implement it. Consuming less red meat is a simple way to use less energy and be healthier.

What is your legacy?

Most living creatures don't soil their nests. Trees fertilize the soil by dropping leaves, bark and limbs. Animals leave manure to enrich the earth. The lives of plants and animals enhance the ecosystem. Humans in the industrialized world have the opposite impact. Our daily activities tend to destroy the ecosystem.

Start at home with a family meeting and ideas from *The Low Carbon Handbook* to reduce-recycle-reuse-refuse-revise. Many people *say* they are willing to be inconvenienced for the sake of leaving a healthier planet for children and grandchildren. *The Low Carbon Diet* is a guide to take baby steps towards sustainability.

Tune up your bikes and ride them to soccer games this weekend. Outfit bikes with lights so it's safe to use them at night. Carpool to the next sport tournament or school meeting. Make Meatless Mondays a new habit. Start a recipe collection of vegetarian family favorites. Set up family work days to insulate pipes and build a chicken coop together. Encourage children to take short jaunts independently by biking, walking or taking public transit.

New practice: Put "sustainability" on your family meeting agenda for the next six months and enlist your family in making changes they propose.

Challenge: Invite friends and neighbors to tackle *The Low Carbon Diet* together. Have a competition to see who can lose the most pounds of carbon.

Super-challenge: Advocate for systemic changes in the communities where you live, play, go to school, worship and work. Start or join a community group to revamp our systems to promote a local lifestyle.

For discussion or journaling: Are you leaving the environment clean enough for your offspring to survive? How are you willing to be inconvenienced for your descendants? What will motivate you to go from thinking about sustainability to taking action?

Key points from Green Chores

- The goals of reduce-recycle-reuse-refuse-revise provide myriad chores for families while reducing your carbon footprint and saving money.
- Children are safer than the media leads us to believe. The possibility of being kidnapped by a stranger is one in 1.5 million.
- Most youngsters who disappear either run away or are taken by an estranged relative.
- Encourage children to walk, bike and take public transit when they have the confidence to so. Form carpools.
- Bicycling can save the planet. Get a bike for everyone in your family and use them for transportation and recreation.
- Plant a few vegetables outside every summer.
- Consider raising backyard chickens, or start a neighborhood egg cooperative.
- Encourage children to raise their own vegetables and chickens.
- Go on a low carbon diet.

What is the purpose to running around like mad?
Where are you running to?
Eckhart Tolle

15
Human *Doing*
or Human *Being?*

M others are some of the most incredible people on the planet. We have a reputation for being self-sacrificing, giving and loving. Attribute our selfless martyrdom to hormones. When I held my firstborn, I instinctively felt overwhelmed to protect and nurture her.

That hormonal command helped me to understand the hormonal directive experienced by men. Theirs is to procreate, ours is to nurture. By some miracle, our hormonal drives intersect for the good of the human race. Many men fall asleep after procreating. The good ones stick around and take on the challenge to support and raise children.

Women are fierce warriors when it comes to protecting our helpless, naïve and vulnerable offspring. Some have waited a long time to become a mother. We understand the influence of our role and dedicate everything we have to it

That can be the problem. We give everything we have to our families and keep nothing for ourselves. We forget ourselves, and depression may set in. After birthing four children born in seven years, I experienced depression and can understand the desperation of child abuse. It takes a village to raise a child.

My mother said, **"A happy mother equals happy breast milk and a happy baby."** As children age, the formula becomes "Happy mothers equal happy families." An important chore for mothers is self-care.

When I ignored my own needs for the sake of my family, I felt resentful, irritable and depressed. The Super-Mom myth is not restricted to employed mothers. As a domo-guru, I made the mistake of over-committing myself as a super-volunteer in addition to everything I did at home. I became a human *doing* instead of a human being.

I went to therapy and workshops to remember to set aside "me-time." I joined a women's book club that met one Friday night a month and went away for the weekend twice a year. Even though we often talked about our families, we took regular breaks from them.

The weekend excursions were not fancy or far away, but they were away. The Wild Women Don't Get the Blues Book Group reminded me that I still had an identity outside of my family. We laughed, cried and had fun together. Book group events gave our husbands an opportunity to be with their children without mom. They managed and it was good for everyone.

At different times, I took piano lessons as an adult, had a weekly tennis game with friends and signed up for courses. Some employed moms are better about self-care than full-time domo-gurus because they are used to leaving their children with others.

Women often feel guilty no matter what we do or don't do for ourselves and others. **Ignore the guilt.** Schedule regular "me time" and marriage dates.

Warning: women who forget about themselves and sacrifice for their family risk becoming depressed. Take the case of Melissa, 30, mother of a nursing toddler and a 4 year old who attend preschool three mornings a week. Melissa's husband works twelve-hour days, including a lengthy commute, while she is the domo-guru. The toddler didn't have her own room so she slept in her parents' bed where her brother often joined them.

Melissa never hired babysitters. "I don't know how to find a babysitter," she told me. Her nearest relatives were thousands of miles away. Melissa had no support system and few breaks from the children, either alone or with her husband.

Melissa had sacrificed everything for the children and forgotten about her own needs. When she came to me for coaching, we realized she had fallen into a depression.

"I don't feel like doing anything. I don't even want to have sex anymore, and I feel guilty about that. The house is a wreck and I always feel a step behind the housework." Melissa said.

The disarray of her house reflected the disarray of her soul.

"I'm short with the children and they often run all over me," Melissa said. The children were accustomed to having her at their service. She had poor boundaries with them. They interrupted her during the few phone calls and visits she had with friends.

I proposed Melissa go out weekly without the children and do something she enjoyed. Melissa enrolled in a power yoga class on Saturday morning and arranged to rendezvous with a new friend one Sunday afternoon a month to quilt together at the friend's house.

I recommended she bring chocolate to the quilting sessions. After a few months of this regime, Melissa began to perk up. She eagerly anticipated the "me time."

Melissa realized it was time to wean her daughter at 22 months so she could learn to get to sleep when Melissa wasn't available. Melissa took my suggestion and moved her husband's home office to the basement to create a bedroom for the toddler, and expected her to use it.

I gave Melissa the assignment to find neighborhood babysitters by calling a nearby church or going to a bus stop to meet middle school students and their parents. Middle-school-age babysitters are more

---

Happy mothers = happy children

When women do not take of ourselves, we are not available to take care of others.

Don't buy into the Super-Mom myth unless you want to be a tired, resentful and cranky martyr. Lower your standards and get help.

Spend time and money on yourself on a regular basis, and arrange for childcare.

motivated, affordable and focused on the children than older teens and adult babysitters.

Melissa eventually found some young babysitters. She and her husband started going out on dates, something they had abandoned when the children arrived. Melissa's depression lifted when she made these changes, especially by scheduling "me time." Melissa felt better and became a better mother and wife. Taking care of herself first benefited everyone.

Energize yourself and your marriage

Preserving yourself is the number one priority. Like the airlines advise during preflight instructions, "Put your oxygen mask on before putting on children's" because if you can't breathe, you can't take care of children.

Likewise, if you're married, give "oxygen" to your marriage regularly. If you have a spouse worth keeping, she or he will be around much longer than the children. Devoting time, energy and fun to a marriage is the best investment a family can make. Call it a chore if it makes you do it.

American marriage statistics are not encouraging. By the time children graduate from high school, about half will end up with divorced parents. Single women with children are the largest poverty group in America, if not the world.

If you loved your spouse enough to get married, do your best to stay connected to whatever brought you together. Don't wait until your relationship has drifted so far from shore that the marriage can't be saved no matter how hard you swim.

The storms of the first twenty years are the most difficult to weather because of the challenges of children, careers and youth. If you can keep a steady course during the first two decades, the next forty years can be very rewarding and all the sweeter if you raised your children together.

Chores: a quick hit of anti-entitlement

Chores do not have to take a lot of time. Children do not have to do a lot of chores to counter entitlement and build a family bond. Even wealthy busy families can figure out a way to work chores into regular routines.

Don, Karen and their children, Jacob, 15 and Emily, 12, live in a million-dollar house within sight of the beach in southern California. They hire housecleaners and gardeners. Money is not a worry.

Don and Karen grew up with servants. Her parents had a housekeeper and a live-in cook. His family had a housekeeper. However, Don and Karen's parents taught them a work ethic through childhood chores, a tradition they have kept with their children.

Jacob and Emily set the table and wash the dinner dishes almost every night, do their own laundry and help out when asked. They don't do a lot around the house, but they do something regularly for the common good.

If one of the teens occasionally wants a day off, Don is flexible. "Everybody is allowed to have a bad day. If they're doing the dishes 98 percent of the time, I am not going to get on their case the other 2 percent," Don said.

Don and Karen are mindful in how they present the jobs. "Who wants to do a *chore?* What you say and how you say it is important. My approach is 'Here's what we're going to do today, and here's how I need your help,'" Don said.

Allowances are not tied to chores or grades. "They receive an allowance because they're part of our family. They do not get paid for grades. That achievement has to come from within. They have to develop the desire to

---

What is affluenza worth?

If your family life is too hectic to incorporate a few chores a week, reconsider the decisions you've made about work, time, money and outside activities.

Research has shown that once people have accumulated enough wealth and income to meet essential daily needs, there is no increase in happiness when income goes up.

My husband Bob found this to be true when he left corporate America in 2004. Our income went down significantly and our quality of life, especially his, soared because he had more time and less stress.

You may want to figure out how to stop **doing** so much and remember how **to be.**

do well at school from within, and hone it themselves," said Don.

Don sometimes works beside his children to motivate them. "One night I wanted the dishes done fast so we could go out after dinner. Instead of harassing them from the sidelines, I worked with them and we finished in ten minutes," said Don, an entrepreneur who employs sixty-five people in a retail business.

"We do not punish the kids for not doing their jobs. They help out most of the time," said Don. He encourages their independence.

"I ride my bike one mile to school and see most of the other kids get dropped off in an SUV," said Jacob with disdain. "It's mostly uphill on the way to school. I don't mind. I like riding my bike."

Don and Karen established a respectful family environment. Their children contribute regularly without being paid or praised. No matter what a family's income, chores are valuable and easily assimilated into a family's daily routine, with a **minimal time investment.**

Slow down with a pajama day

We all have the same twenty-four hours in a day. How we spend it depends on our values, attitude and need for outside activities. Pajama days are excellent ways to transform from human *doings* to human *beings.*

Children often like staying home. It's the parents who seek the outside stimulation. Children thrive on routine and open-ended play time, which has shrunk by one-third in recent years, according to Susan Linn, author of *The Case for Make-Believe: Saving Play in a Commercialized World.*

Playtime provides children opportunities to solve problems, work out worries, and comprehend the complexities of the world through role-playing, imagination and fantasy. Play provides rich opportunities for self-growth, self-awareness and healing, according to Linn. Children need open-ended playtime. It's adults who don't have the patience and ability to hang out at home without sugared screen time.

When my gang was under 10, their favorite way to spend a Saturday morning was a pajama day. They stayed in pajamas and built forts out of blankets, card tables and couch cushions. They emptied the cupboards of every truck, doll and game. Casey, the eldest, arranged and solemnized marriages, set up housekeeping, established schools and planned for holidays. Noah got married dozens of times.

Rehearsal for Christmas began in earnest in September. Even the dog reveled in pajama days by nestling amid piles of blankets, pillows and toys.

They loved pajama days. I liked watching them create an imaginary world.

I surrendered to chaos for three or four hours and planned at least fifteen minutes of cleanup with them, a small investment for a big payoff. They enjoyed playing with each other and it freed up some time for me.

Pajama days are good for children who are always on the go. It's akin to the slow family movement. Pajama days allow children to reclaim some unstructured playtime without adult interference.

Invite a friend or cousin to a pajama morning, for only children or siblings with a large gap in ages.

Parents and children may need to develop the ability to stay at home, at risk of boredom.

Low key, low cost, good fun

Some of my favorite ways to unwind with children include the following.

A climbing tree.

A playhouse or tree house.

A fireside picnic.

A bubbling creek -- bring water shoes or old sneakers, a lunch, a book to read a friends. Let children explore and get wet and dirty.

Let them eat lunch outside in a high place like a tree or swing set.

Provide a refrigerator box to play in and decorate.

Sing and make music together.

Cook something ambitious.

Stay at a playground for a long while.

Visit a train station.

Revel in mud, puddles and snow.

Pick wild berries.

Plant seeds and flowers.

Grow a few backyard vegetables.

Hike a small hill, not more than forty-five minutes up.

Take long walks in conservation land or in big parks nearby.

Canoe on a river or lake.

Visit the ocean, pond or a lake, no explanation or toys needed, just get out of the way.

Ask children for ideas and do them.

Pajama days counteract activity mania

My children reveled in pajama days with each other while Bob and I amused ourselves at home. We eschewed affluenza on weekends and the grind of year-round sports competitions. For peace of family, my children were limited to studying one musical instrument and participating in one sport in the fall and spring. We took off summer and winter from the grind of youth sports.

Some years, we participated in 4-H and scouts. Even this amount of activity was barely manageable. We skied together in winter, just for fun with no competition. Summer was for adventures and visiting relatives. We enjoyed being home, working on projects, doing home maintenance, being together, and going on trips.

Beware of family-busters

When Noah was 9, he asked to swim on an indoor winter swimming team. I said yes, and then realized it was a family-buster. I would be spending Saturday or Sunday chauffeuring Noah to swim meets, in addition to three practices a week. I would sit on bleachers on weekends, steaming and sweating, while Noah waited to swim in three 59-second races. That's not a normal childhood or family experience.

Some parents sacrifice normal family life in the quest for super-achievers. A 25-year old female wrote in my survey, "I spent my life in the gym doing gymnastics. I have almost no memories of family dinner since I was at the gym from 3:30 to 7:30, five days a week from ages 6 to 12."

Many parents who engage in the sports-centered lifestyle have convinced themselves and their children that the kids love it. The children don't know anything else. They've never been expected to creatively entertain themselves on a Saturday, to feel boredom, to mow the lawn, dawdle in their room or have the freedom to splash flour and sugar on the kitchen floor while making cookies from scratch.

Children ARE interruptions

Parents often whine, "I can't get anything done" when their progeny are around. Some modern parents are not used to spending extended time with children because the children have been raised in daycare, and consider being with children as "work."

Some parents are unable to relax or do something else when in the presence of their children and have not cultivated the art of being interrupted.

My friend Rich stood ankle deep in our pond while his preschoolers frolicked in the water.

"Do you want a beer?" I said.

"No," Rich said, watching his children anxiously.

I brought out an adult float for Rich to put his feet up, with a compartment for a cold drink.

"Here, Rich take a load off," I said, and pushed the float towards him.

Rich ignored me and said, "Hey kids, try this." They clambered aboard the float, which was not meant for children to stand on. I grimaced, puzzled why Rich couldn't relax while keeping half-an-eye on his toddlers.

Like many parents, Rich needs practice expecting his children to entertain each other, with him in the background. Rich must master the fine art of interruption, and parallel play. **Children can learn to play independently while parents are nearby, doing something else.**

The most difficult professions are when the worker is constantly interrupted. Most typical women's work is punctuated by constant interruption including administrative assistants, nurses, teachers, flight attendants and especially domo-gurus. Any occupation oriented toward taking care of people usually involves regular interruptions.

Whose problem is boredom?

One time, a child said to me, "I'm bored." I permanently solved their lack of imagination. I said: "Help make dinner. Sweep the floor. Vacuum, pick up toys, dust or weed the yard."

Children are responsible to entertain themselves. Too many parents become servants to their children by assuming the job of entertaining children when they whine, "I'm bored." **Put them to work if they turn to you to solve their lack of imagination.**

Like failure, boredom offers opportunity. Boredom allows children to discover their inner resources, follow their whim and solve problems.

203

When children are allowed to feel empty and still without sugared-screen-time, they will eventually connect to their creativity, call a friend or take a nap.

Parents don't touch this problem, except to offer chores as a way to solve the boredom. Avoid the temptation to entertain or relent to additional screen time to cure boredom. Even babies can learn to amuse themselves for fifteen to thirty minutes when parents allow them. Such unstructured playtime is essential to their growth and development.

The Zen of 39 dirty windows

I learned the art of interruption out of necessity when we bought a neglected old house when the children were 4, 2, and 7 months old. The thirty-nine windows hadn't been washed in at least a decade. Maybe this book could be called "Dirty windows teach life lessons."

My strategy was to put the baby down for his morning nap and have window-cleaning supplies ready to go during one hour of public television. TV and DVDs have value when used in moderation.

I cleaned three windows an hour and checked on them every fifteen minutes. If they continued to sleep and play peacefully for another fifteen or twenty minutes, I started another window. After sixty or eighty minutes, I joined them on the floor for ten minutes of undivided attention, or silently watched them. It took almost a month to clean all the windows. The project was constantly interrupted.

We used the same tactic when renovating the house. I was on-call for

---

Find frugal local fun in nature

Gabe felt badly he didn't have $100 to take his son, 12, to an amusement park in the summer. Instead, they went fishing at a neighborhood pond, with a picnic lunch and spent a Sunday afternoon together.

Gabe taught his son how to bait the hook and paddle a canoe they had borrowed. His son enjoyed the day and the father-son bonding. Gabe still felt guilty and remorseful he couldn't provide "real" entertainment for his son at the amusement park.

---

interruptions while we converted an attic into a master bedroom suite, with three children under age 6. Occasionally I gave them jobs to do, like sanding drywall or painting a radiator. Even if they only did it for a few minutes, it reinforced the idea that their contributions were appreciated. I worked in small installments and supported Bob with meals and childcare. After many interruptions, we finished the room.

Before becoming a mother, I had no patience for interruptions. I had to focus on one thing, without stopping, until it was finished. That changed after the children were born. Children are magnificent teachers.

Avoid nurturing human *doings*

Constantly interfering with a child's playtime by entertaining him or enrolling him in non-stop activities creates human doings instead of human beings.

Mowing lawns as a tonic for boredom

It was a Tuesday morning during summer vacation in 1985. I was 13 and my brother Chad was 12. My father came into the house and found us watching TV.

In a disgusted tone he said "What on earth would possess you two to be inside watching TV?"

"We're bored," I said casually.

He called the City of Grangeville, Idaho where we lived, (population 3,500) and got a list of all the overgrown and abandoned lawns.

"My children will be mowing them for free," my father told the city official.

And we did, all summer long.

We did not get paid for mowing lawns that summer. My Dad still thinks this was an absolute stroke of genius on his part and makes an evil laugh when I tell the story.

To this day, I refuse to utter the word "bored." My brother Chad still loves to mow lawns.

Kim Parsells   Lewiston, Idaho
Founder of an Internet marketing company--www.surfisup.com

Human doings miss out on the *being* of life. They become consumers and performers instead of creators and risk-takers. They depend on having experiences created for them, and people waiting on them, such as teachers, coaches, nannies, day care providers and even recess leaders. Human doings have little experience of how to create or fix things, or solve problems because of the frenzy to perform, go to the next activity and buy more things.

Discover the Zen in reveling in an open day with no agenda. Watch children engaged in pretend play. Swing in the hammock. Read a book.

Slow down and discover the Zen in doing things together , such as raking leaves, baking bread, making jam, caring for a pet, planting seeds, sewing doll clothes, knitting, playing cards, building a tree house, looking for frogs in a creek, and even cleaning a toilet.

Slow down and allow children to connect and contribute to their first community of their family. Being part of a community requires contributions, which come naturally when families spend time working, relaxing and playing at home.

Calm the frenzy and take a break from activity mania and affluenza. Slow down, get out of the SUV on a Saturday and have a pajama day.

Family time instead of sports time

If your family can't find time for a few family meetings a month, time to do the dishes together at night, or an hour a week to work together, ask, "Are my children overscheduled?"

As an experiment, take off one season from organized sports and experience the leisure of a family dinner not dominated by a practice schedule. Travel youth sports, cheerleading, scouting, dance and a hundred other activities can erode family life. Re-learn how to be, without an agenda. Allow boredom. If they can't solve it, put them to work.

Parents enroll toddlers in diapers into organized activities, or feel guilty if their preschoolers don't get a head-start on organized lessons for music, gymnastics, dance, swimming lessons and even yoga.

Parents want children to be experts by age 5. The time could be better spent playing with them and mastering the art of interruption. Toddlers don't need professionals to lead their exploration of the world. Parents can sing songs, play in the yard, crank up the stereo and dance in the family room, splash in a pool, run around the yard, play ball and wrestle together on the floor.

Let siblings work it out

To create a harmonious home and have successful pajama days, teach children how to get along by allowing them to work out differences. This requires time for training, encouragement, discussing it at family meetings and using natural and logical consequences.

I can hear objections shouting out as you read this. "The younger one needs my protection." "They might hurt or kill each other." "There's no way they can be in the same room without killing each other."

All of those expectations will be true as long as parents intervene in sibling disagreements and don't give children the time and space to work things out.

If you have an older and a younger child, I bet your younger child knows how to defend himself and get back at the older child. The baby always has tactics at his disposal, despite a smaller size and maturity.

When children are allowed to work it out, they discover fighting hurts. Younger and smaller children learn that it's dangerous to tangle with bigger, older and smarter siblings, unless they can count on a parent to be a body guard, lawyer and judge.

When my two sons, seventeen months apart, wanted to battle, the rule was "go to the basement or outside." The disputes ended quickly without an audience, heat or light. It helped they were of similar stature.

If parents must intervene, don't take sides and apply the same outcome to everyone involved. For example, if children are fighting over a toy, remove the toy. If children can't agree on what TV show to watch, turn off the TV.

Make encouraging neutral statements: "I'm sure you can work it out." Rewarding tattle tales will keep parents busy and involved and deny children the opportunity to learn negotiation and survival skills.

There are many benefits to children being put in the same boat and being allowed to work out their problems. They become closer, easier to care for, and more resourceful, resilient and responsible.

New practice: Withdraw from activity mania by staying home one Saturday morning a month. Let children stay in pajamas, with no electronics, and give permission to make a mess. Don't interfere. If they protest, "I'm bored," offer a choice of chores. Check on them every half hour and encourage their efforts.

Challenge: Evaluate the pace of your family's lifestyle and determine if a change course is needed. As a trial, drop out of organized activities for three months and do something together on one weekend day.

For discussion or journaling: Describe childhood memories of unstructured playtime. How have you re-created such opportunities for your children?

Key points for *Human doing or human being?*

- Maximize the amount of time parents are available to raise children and minimize outside work time, if possible.
- Ensure that the domo-guru (primary caregiver) makes self-care a chore of high priority.
- If married, make it a chore to schedule dates without children. Maintain the investment in your marriage.
- If you're a human *doing*, work on transitioning to a human *being* again. Evaluate your schedule and figure out what to quit and create some free time.
- Solve children's boredom by giving them chores.
- Children don't need to be scheduled every minute of every day. Parents do. Children thrive on open-ended play time.
- Parents can master the art of interruption and learn to relax or work while children amuse themselves.
- Let children work out their differences by not interfering and by putting them all on the same team, regardless of ages.
- If your family doesn't have time for monthly family meetings a and to do a few chores, evaluate the lifestyle choices you've made and consider alternatives.

---

*The trouble with learning to parent on the job
is that your child is the teacher.*
Robert Brault

16
You are not my Mother:
Blended Families

E mma, 6, never lets her stepfather Ben forget that he is an interloper. "Every time we sit down to a meal, play a game or talk, Emma says, 'Mom, you go first, then me. Then Ben goes last,'" Ben said.

"Emma asks, 'Mommy, can we go talk someplace *without* Ben?' If I offer to help her with something, all I hear is, 'I don't want you to do it, only Mommy can.' Emma has to be reminded to say 'Good night Ben' or 'Good bye Ben.'

"As much as I want to hug her, comfort her or even just talk to her, she turns away and ignores me. Everything I ask her to do is questioned and immediately taken to her mother to be overruled. On good days we can talk and play a bit together. On bad days, I don't exist. It is not easy at the best of times," Ben said.

Emma has been crowned queen of the roost, a frightening job for a 6-year-old. It is up to her mother to establish a democratic home where Ben isn't relegated in service to the queen.

A simple solution is to hold family meetings in which everyone takes turns running the meetings and going first at games afterwards.

Ben and Emma could benefit from spending time together without Mom. Emma could enjoy some "mom and me" time without Ben.

This next suggestion may sound counter-intuitive. Ben could step back from the relationship and give Emma the space to come to him. It may take years and it may never happen because some children are so hurt by divorce that they take it out on the most convenient adults. The challenge for Ben is to not take the rejection personally and be able to be with eh waiting. In time, Emma will eventually see Ben as the good guy he is.

Ben and Emma are caught in the crossfire of a blended family. The odds are against them. Second marriages with stepchildren have the highest rate of failure. Step-parents are often treated like second-class citizens in their own homes.

For example, Ramona has been a stepmother to Brittany since she was 4 years old. Because Ramona was available during the day, she has attended most of Brittany's parent-teacher conferences and volunteered to lead one of Brittany's after school activities. Now a teen, Brittany has never been affectionate, accepting or appreciative of Ramona. With maturity, Brittany will see Ramona for who she is and the contributions she made to her life.

Step-parents like Ben and Ramona deserve credit for their commitment to the blended family and willingness to be a target of children's anger, pain and immaturity.

Ben is not alone in his quest for equal rights. When Aiesha's stepchildren demanded to ride in the front seat next to their father (who was driving) when they went places, Aiesha came up with a solution.

"You ride in the front on the way there, and I get to sit next to him on the way home," said Aiesha in a fair compromise. Children gravitate towards fairness. They understand how to take turns.

Creativity, flexibility and equal rights are essential tenets to smooth the rifts of blended families.

Divided we fall

It's essential for the adults in blended families to form a united front. Traditional families benefit from a united front, but step-parents in particular must work from the same playbook. Here are some suggestions.

1. Hold weekly family meetings followed by family fun in which the adults compete enthusiastically. Games are an excellent way to level the playing field and build relationships.

2. Prepare, eat and cleanup dinner together at least three times a week.

3. Establish new traditions. Go camping one long weekend a year; clean the house and maintain the lawn together; plan annual events like picking apples at the same orchard or going to the beach or a park; establish new ways to celebrate holidays; have an annual barbecue; host an annual fun outdoor competition.

4. Cultivate a sense of humor. Tell jokes and funny stories. Collect jokes and cartoons about blended families and step-parenting. Share them at dinner and family meetings. **If you can't laugh at it, you can't live with it.**

5. Allow youngsters of all ages to work out problems without adult intervention. Act like a consultant. Ask questions to help them solve it.

6. Parents **must** set the tone of teamwork. Children instantly spot uncertainty and exploit disagreements. Don't take sides or play the game, "Ask your Mom," or "Ask your Dad."

7. Seek outside help when necessary. Don't drift so far from shore that it's impossible to swim back.

8. Honor yourselves. A blended family has double the uncontrollable variables of a typical family. Use this book as a guide for a positive parenting plan.

Create a welcoming atmosphere

For forty years, my parents welcomed a stream of new boyfriends, girlfriends, in-laws, and grandchildren into our family. My mother welcomed all of them with affection. She embraced in-laws who were not destined to stay long and advocated they be treated fairly, even if their behavior needed improvement.

Blended families thrive on family meetings

When Anne and her son, Drew, 4, moved in with Brian and his children Margo, 8, and Matt, 6, they held weekly family meetings for a year to ease the transition.

"Everyone would get a turn to discuss what wasn't working. We started at my left and went around the circle. When they figured that out, they would race to get the seat on my left to be the first to have their issue heard," Anne said.

They used this format: "I feel hurt by you when," and "I feel most loved by you when." Anne started with the "hurts" and finished with the "love."

For example, Matt said, "I feel hurt by Drew when he doesn't ask permission to use my toys."

Later in the meeting, Matt will have to say something unrelated to the problem, like, "I feel most appreciated by Drew when he shares his candy with me."

The meetings were useful when Anne and Brian combined households. "In the beginning, there was a lot of 'You're not my dad,' and 'You're not my mom,'" Anne said.

The family meetings helped to build trust. "We learned about each other and how to communicate. The kids wrote their issues on the family meeting agenda on the fridge. It was cute to see 6-year-old handwriting saying, 'Drew used my toys,'" Anne said.

"In the beginning, there were a lot of issues to resolve because the kids were not getting along. After six or eight months and we knew each other better, family meetings were a great place to bring up new ideas. The kids suggested we shut off the TV and play games tell stories and jokes for two hours, and have an upside-down dinner with dessert first," Anne said.

Anne and Brian allowed the children to work out their problems with minimal interference.

"I was often the mediator. I was not the problem-solver. Most of the time, we let them work it out," Anne said.

Mildred modeled how to welcome new family members. She never reminded us that we were "her children." She showed that by regularly siding with my husband. Mildred stayed in touch with a former daughter-in-law for years after she and my brother divorced.

Mildred used finesse and set the tone in the same way blended families can do. Adults have the onus to rise above the fracas, especially if the families include teens that are under the influence of hormones.

Blended families bring pain and regret from previous relationships. Alliances and history run deep, so it may take years for a step-parent to build trust with their partner's children. Step-parents must let go of the outcome. When a child directs anger at a step-parent, she is showing trust in the adult. Unlikely as it may seem, that trust is a start to a relationship.

Use family meetings

Keep an open family meeting agenda on the fridge. Discuss recurring conflicts, even if a resolution seems unlikely. Just being heard can allow steam to escape and bring relief.

Many problems have no solution, as shown in our family meeting annals in which Ian annoyed his older sister Casey for several years. Casey regularly put complaints about Ian on the agenda

When Casey was 11 and Ian was 7, the minutes written by Noah, 9, read, "Chewing things. Ian has been chewing on Casey's fork. We all make mistakes."

Three months later, "Casey says Ian asks dumb questions continuously" while doing dishes. The suggestions include the following.

1. Don't ask dumb questions.
2. Don't answer questions.
3. Talk about something else.
4. Concentrate on dishes.
5. Earplugs.
6. Go to room.
7. Sing songs.
8. Play loud music to listen to.
   Table until next week.

The issue was never discussed again or resolved until Ian matured. He and Casey get along well today.

Parents can set an example and write issues on the family meeting agenda, such as, "Casey's backpack—Dad" to discuss the problem of Casey leaving her backpack in the middle of the floor. Or, "Dishes—Mom." I often put this item on the agenda. I think their resistance was a form of rebellion. I'm grateful if not putting away the drying year after year, despite my vociferous complaints, was the worst of their rebellion.

Allow the family meeting facilitator to run discussions of the agenda items. The suggestions from children will be entertaining and practical.

The flow of family bonding

One day the toilet stopped flushing in the bathroom shared by Kristen, 12, and Jayla, 15, a foreign exchange student from Senegal we hosted for a school year.

The girls did not tell me or Bob and continued to add urine and toilet paper. When the bathroom began to smell, I investigated and thought, *Whose problem is it?*

The stinky toilet was a family problem because the smell permeated the upstairs. Our bedroom was adjacent to the bathroom. It was Kristen and Jayla's problem because they used that bathroom exclusively.

Someone had to fish out the pile of toilet paper in order for Bob to fix

---

Practice acceptance

Mark and Deb each brought two children to their new family. The youngest three got along well and went to the same school.

Mark's oldest daughter, Kaitlyn, was in college when the family got together. Kaitlyn's sexual preference rankled Deb, especially when Kaitlyn came home from college for the summer and shared a room with her girlfriend. Deb's body negative language was easily interpreted by the rest of the family.

Deb's attitude towards the situation caused a deep rift, one of many that eventually caused the fragile family to break up. Blended families in particular must respect each other's decisions and withhold judgment. Even if Deb did not approve, she could have been aware of maintaining neutral body language.

---

the toilet. When I discovered the problem at 9:30 p.m., I said, "Jayla, pick out the toilet paper and put it in this bag," and handed her a plastic bag. Kristen was already asleep.

"Gross! I'm not going to stick my hand in the toilet." Jayla was adamant, horrified and upset.

"I don't want to put my hand in there either. You put it there. You can take it out," I said. It was not my toilet paper.

Jayla was so upset that she called her mother in Senegal the next day.

The natural consequence of adding toilet paper to a broken toilet is that someone must remove it. My mistake was to not involve Kristen in extricating the toilet paper. It was not fair to Jayla.

We managed to repair the relationship and the toilet. **That's how long-term relationships succeed – by constant repair.** No relationship is trustworthy until it has been tested by a crisis, anger and conflict.

A few weeks later that spring, water provided another bonding opportunity for Kristen and Jayla, who had kept their distance from each other because of the three-year age difference.

The basement flooded when the winter snow melted quickly because the house was built next to a wetland.

When two inches of water swelled in the basement, I put Kristen and Jayla to work sweeping water to the drain. I worked with them for a short time and encouraged them by saying, "Thanks for sweeping the water. There is a ton of water here. It would have been hard to do this alone. I appreciate you finishing while I go to work."

After the water crisis, I discerned a shift in Jayla and Kristen's relationship. Previously, Jayla had disdained Kristen as the younger and less savvy sibling. Cleaning up two inches of water brought them closer together.

Incorporating Jayla into our house was simpler than a blended family because Jayla did not come with a parent. We expected Jayla to conform to our system.

Blended families demand more negotiation and discussion. Think of a blended family like a merged corporation. A lot of meetings are required in the beginning until everyone finds a new place to belong. Remembering Adler's theory, we all crave a place to belong.

Yours, mine and ours

When Peggy was 10 years old her mother died. Her brother was 12. Two years later, Peggy's father Barry married Stephanie, after being introduced by their dead mother's sister.

"My aunt wanted us to be a whole family again," Peggy said, even though her father had been widowed for a short time. Stephanie brought her children, 4 and 2 years old, to the blended family. Her husband had died.

"Suddenly I was a big sister and our house went from being silent and subdued to being really lively. The kids were too young to recognize they had lost a father. My brother and I were old enough to know the loss of a parent," Peggy said. "We went back to being a traditional family with two parents, doing things as a family that we weren't able to do when my father was working and taking care of us."

The family got even livelier. "A number of years later, my father and mother had a baby. I was 16 and my brother was 18 when our youngest sister was born. The family became that much larger and crazier. That was the pinnacle of blending the family," Peggy said.

Today, Peggy's family prioritizes their traditions and gatherings. "We stayed close as we got older and left home. As our younger siblings grew older, we intentionally got together, especially for holidays. We all come from different places for Thanksgiving, Rosh Hashanah, Hanukah and Passover. My mother made sure all of the holidays were at their home.

"I never called Stephanie my stepmother. That was not part of our language. She became my mother and I was glad to have her," Peggy said.

Peggy's blended family is important to them, perhaps more than a traditional family. "We stay in touch as a family.

"We are a very functional family. We don't have siblings who are mad at each other or who are not talking to each other. So many friends refer to themselves as coming from a 'dysfunctional family.' It never crossed my mind that we were a dysfunctional family. We are intentional about being happy that we are a family, something we appreciate because of losing my birth mother at young age," Peggy said.

The challenge of blended families

Like underdogs must try harder, blended families must try harder. The parents in a blended family can benefit from crafting a positive parenting plan by using this book to work from the same game plan.

Typical families will benefit from the Adlerian approach; it can propel blended families towards long-term success because it provides a positive parenting plan.

New practice: Regularly hold family dinners, meetings, fun and work sessions. Ignore protests and absences. Invite everyone and expect them to attend. Make it as fun as possible and give a role to all who show up.

Challenge: Put yours-mine-and-ours in the same boat and let them work it out. Solve conflicts by using encouragement and family meetings. Act like a consultant to avoid being the cop, judge and security guard.

For discussion or journaling: How are the new practices developing patience, forgiveness, acceptance and appreciation in you?

Key points from
***You are not my Mother:* Blended Families**

- Build cohesion for a blended family through regular family meetings, dinners, household chores, playtime and new seasonal and holiday traditions.

- Go camping at least once a year if possible.

- Parents must present a unified front and establish a democratic household.

- Both parents commit to the same positive parenting plan.

- The adults must rise above the situation and practice patience, forgiveness and acceptance. Step-parents can expect rough waters. Hang on, have hope and show maturity by not taking it personally.

- Allow the children to work out their disagreements. It is more effective than intervening.

A misbehaving child is a discouraged child.
Rudolf Dreikurs

17
Name It and Tame It

'Henry will be in your class in January," said Nancy Kelly's fellow teachers at the middle school where she teaches art. "He's a real handful," they warned.

On the first day of the new term Henry lived up to his reputation. While Nancy wrote on the blackboard and explained the art project for the day, strange sounds came from Henry's corner of the classroom.

"Moooo. Quack, quack, quack. Oink – snuffle – oink."

Nancy stopped writing, turned to the class and said, "I think I hear animal noises."

Henry and his pals snickered with the rest of the class.

Nancy looked straight at the likely culprits and said, "I can make animal noises, too."

"*You* can make animal noises, Mrs. Kelly?" Henry said.

"Yes. I can make animal noises. But I don't make them in class. I make animal noises in appropriate places."

"Can you *really* make animal noises, Mrs. Kelly? Would you make some for us?" Henry said enthusiastically.

"I will make animal noises for you *if* you sign an agreement that you will never make another animal noise in my classroom for the rest of the term," Nancy said.

Nancy drafted the agreement which Henry signed immediately in anticipation of Nancy's animal noises.

With the promise in writing, Nancy bent over, dropped her arms straight down, clasped her hands at her knees, and slowly swung her trunk back and forth. She leaned back slowly, pointed her hands to the ceiling and trumpeted.

The class cheered. She was a very good elephant.

They were ready for the second act. Nancy played it up and paused before making an endearing "Quack, quack, quack" that sounded like a real duck. After her antics they returned to the day's lesson.

Nancy's creative response to Henry sidestepped what could have become a semester-long problem.

Instead, Nancy won his cooperation through creativity and mutual respect. She avoided giving Henry undue attention.

Nancy did all of this without getting angry or threatening Henry with punishment. Nancy invested a few minutes of time for training with Henry. She did the unexpected, didn't take Henry or herself too seriously and created a positive learning environment.

Henry walked away feeling respected, heard and empowered. It is a stellar story of how to respond differently to children.

Becoming aware of a child's unconscious goals is the first step for parents and teachers to change their response.

Adler and Dreikurs identified the four mistaken goals of behavior as the desire for undue attention, the struggle for power, revenge, and helplessness.

Children are unconscious to these goals and must never be told by parents about them. It will not serve the situation to tell children about the mistaken goals they are acting out. Parents must keep this knowledge confidential.

Let's look at each of the four goals in depth.

Goal 1: The desire for constant attention

Henry mistakenly believed, "I count only when I'm the center of attention." Such attention can be garnered by being cute, funny, clever and charming, or by hurting others, stealing, and other anti-social behavior.

At home, younger children may act out by using water power: spilling milk, wetting their pants or crying, or other tactics to interrupt parents to get their need for attention met.

Children need attention regularly like a plant needs water. We must judge the quantity and appropriateness of that attention. Parents can put positive attention in the "bank," catch them being good, encourage them, then expect the child to play independently, go to bed, eat dinner, or do what they're supposed to do.

Like Nancy demonstrated, investing in a few moments of animal noises paid off in a semester of peace and respect from Henry.

Children will get their needs met through positive or negative attention. We want to avoid soggy potato chips and regularly give them nice fresh crisp potato chips. Parents must spend time with children. The question is, how much attention and when?

Yielding to excessive demands for misbehavior may reinforce a child's negative self concept and could make the matter worse. Parents can make the situation worse by using reward and punishment. It convinces the child bad behavior is the only way to get his needs met, according to Dreikurs.

The pinnacle of attention is to be simultaneously touched, looked at and spoken to. When a parent yells and hits a child, the parent is talking to, looking at and touching the child. It's better than being ignored. At least the child exists in the eyes of the parent.

The foundation of Adler's psychology is that people have a basic desire to belong, to be a part of a family, classroom, gang or group. Belonging is fundamental to human nature. Parents must practice giving their children positive attention and encouragement **before** they ask for it.

When children are short-changed for attention, they'll take a soggy potato chip if they can't get a fresh one.

Goal 2: The struggle for power

The divvying up of power in a home reflects on the parent's maturity, confidence and personal power which take time to develop. As a young mother, I felt threatened by my children's power quest. I got tangled in a power struggle with two of them and felt like the loser when I resorted to yelling, punishment and sometimes hitting my then 5-and 2-year-olds.

The apple doesn't fall far from the tree. As a child, I was famous for my temper tantrums. As a young mother I felt insecure sharing power with my preschoolers. I thought the only solution was to dominate power-questing children, which made matters worse.

I found relief when the study group named it. It was up to me to tame it. **The first hurdle to solve any challenge is to become aware of it.**

Adults must be willing to share a piece of the power pie to empower children, create a peaceful home, and set the foundation for a lifelong relationship. When children are denied power they exploit the backdoors of passive aggression, stonewalling and revenge.

The art of management (power) is to get others to do what we want them to do. Encouragement, family meetings and parents minding their own business are subtle ways to influence others.

Parents must master subtle methods of power, which requires patience. I learned to quietly wait for youngsters to discover their own answers, without saying "I told you so." I can almost avoid thinking it.

What parents *do* and say is as important as what we *don't* do or say, especially in a power struggle.

When a child seeks power, they are feeling threatened and believe the only way to gain power is by controlling others. Instead of going head-to-head, which gets painful and loud, and dangerous with teens, parents can learn to respond differently before anger escalates.

Power-questing children thrive on being offered choices. It gives them a feeling of control. Make sure both choices are acceptable to parents.

Remember that power children often develop into leaders and entrepreneurs. Difficult children often turn out to be the most interesting adults. Casey and I sparred in power struggles for years. Today she is a successful businesswoman and manager.

Bubbles and Shamim

Shamim, 10, was responsible to feed his pet canary Bubbles daily, and clean her cage once a week.

"Shamim, feed Bubbles," his mother Tina called from the kitchen. Shamim was playing video games and ignored his mother.

"Come on, Shamim. You were supposed to do it yesterday and you forgot, as usual. It's time to do it now. Bubbles is your bird. When we got her, you promised to take care of her." There was no response.

"Can you hear me, Shamim?"

Still, no response. Annoyance mounting into anger, Tina stormed into the playroom, put her hands on her hips and shouted, "Turn off that video game NOW and feed Bubbles. It is your responsibility. It's your bird. She is hungry. Take care of her now."

"I'm almost done this level," said Shamim, his eyes never leaving the screen. He was used to ignoring his mother's tirades.

"If you don't take care of this bird, I'll get rid of her, I swear I will," said Tina, her heart pounding.

Shamim kept playing. He had heard this threat many times before and his mother had never acted on it. Shamim had become mother-deaf.

"Do you hear me, Shamim? I will give Bubbles away. Come and feed her now and clean her cage. It smells. You promised to take care of this bird. It's your bird."

"I'll be there in a minute," Shamim said and continued playing.

"I'm going to count to three, if you don't move, I'm going to take away your video games for a week," Tina said, her voice escalating. At this point, some parents might hit the child or yell louder.

Shamim made a few more moves with the controller, set it aside, and said calmly, "That was my best score in a week. I hate cleaning the cage." He went to the kitchen, which was on the way to Bubbles' cage, and stopped for a drink while Tina fumed at the sink.

Change your response

Tina could have sidestepped the power struggle by using a family meeting to agree upon a bird care schedule, then remind Shamim once, give a choice, take action, and avoid anger.

Tina could have said: "Shamim, I see you didn't take care of Bubbles this morning. You promised at the family meeting to clean her cage once a week, by yesterday. The cage smells and she's hungry. Please come and do it now."

If Shamim doesn't respond, she must take action. Tina can say in a firm and pleasant voice, "You didn't take care of Bubbles when it was convenient for you; you have to stop what you're doing now." Tina must turn off the video game.

The more Tina lectures, the more she undermines her own power and trains Shamim to be mother-deaf. Without action, she loses credibility.

To avoid repeating the power struggle and come up with a long-term solution, Tina can put "bird care" on the family meeting agenda. "Care of Bubbles" might appear on the family meeting agenda several times. She can ask Shamim and the family for ideas on how to remember to take care of the bird and repeat the possibility of giving the bird away.

Some solutions include: establish a "bird care routine" and check a chart or calendar upon completion; set Shamim's alarm on a wrist watch or cell phone as a reminder; agree that there is no screen time or snacks until the bird had been taken care of.

Tina can set a date with Shamim to re-evaluate the quality of his bird care. If he must be nagged to care for the bird, the related, respectful and reasonable solution is to give the bird away, a plan Tina must be willing to act on.

Defuse children on a power quest

Parents can realize they're in a power struggle if they are feeling angry and threatened. A power struggle may come after parents have ignored a child's constant antics for attention, or the child needs power to feel secure.

Power-seeking children fear they will lose their self-worth by submitting to parental demands, according to Dreikurs. As children on a power quest get older, they may act out in bigger, louder and more dangerous ways to demonstrate their power.

Before I gave up hitting, threatening and punishing, I sometimes hit them. I felt defeated when provoked into hitting them. I had been reduced to using my superior size and strength to intimidate them.

Another word for that is bullying. Bullied children learn to find power through intimidating others. They may grow up to be batterers, tyrants, bullies, or worse. As children mature into adolescence, power struggles can have dangerous outcomes. Many young bullies have a mentor at home who regularly demonstrates the advantages of superior size and strength to intimidate weaker people into submission. Beware of the day when the

---

The charm of encouragement

I grew up in my family's restaurant business. When I was 4 years old, my father managed a Dunkin' Donuts in Columbia, Missouri. They put me on a milk crate and I frosted and filled doughnuts for fun. I enjoyed "working" because the results were so well-appreciated. My dad said, "You frost the doughnuts better than some of the waitresses."

In 1980, my parents opened a Chinese restaurant. I started by making all the wontons. On busy weekends, my brother and I washed the dishes by hand. We'd get $20 at the end of the night and that was a big deal. I was 10 years old.

As I grew older, my responsibilities increased. In high school, I worked as cashier, host, takeout packer and manager. I still made all the wontons. In the morning before school, I'd make huge vats of soup for the day. I worked through college and didn't quit the restaurant business until I received my degree in journalism and got an internship at The Denver Post.

My two brothers and I resented working at the restaurant at one time or another, because we basically did nothing else. I never went to slumber parties or hung out with friends at the mall. We were also aware that we were lucky to have the experience.

I learned how to: have a work ethic; think on my feet; think about the big picture; not rest on my laurels; be resourceful because we had to find creative low-cost solutions to problems; and to be an entrepreneur.

Hsiao-Ching Chou   Seattle, Washington
Suzuki + Chou Communimedia--www.suzukichoumedia.com

---

tide turns and Junior has gotten his driver's license and grown bigger, and stronger than his mentor.

Five steps to defuse a child on a power quest

1. Give choices, all of them acceptable to parents.
2. Encourage the youth to run family meetings and take the leadership in appropriate family projects and excursions.
3. Refuse to accept their invitation to do the power dance. Provide clear choices, take action with few words, and avoid anger.
4. Practice the enjoyable art of encouragement daily. This will eliminate much negative behavior, build a positive relationship and nurture their self-esteem.
5. Realize their power quest is an asset that can benefit them in school, work and relationships. They may use their personal power to become leaders.

Goal 3: Revenge

Power struggles can escalate into revenge when a child feels hurt, ignored or overpowered and believes the only way to win is to get even. Tots-to-teens use this tactic. It can become lethal as children get older, bigger, stronger, savvier, and have more options.

"Hannah, mow the lawn today," Meg said to her daughter Hannah, 14, on a Saturday morning. Hannah went to the family computer and stayed there until lunchtime, listening to her iPod and text-messaging her friends.

"Hannah, you're grounded for a week if you don't mow the lawn today," Meg said in an angry tone. Hannah ate lunch and went to her room while Meg stewed in frustration.

At 6 p.m., Hannah came downstairs dressed to go out. "Mom, can I have a ride to Brittany's house? We're going to the movies tonight."

Furious, Meg said, "No way, young lady. You were supposed to mow the lawn today. You may not go out. You are grounded for a week."

Hannah yelled back in protest, "It's not fair! I hate mowing the lawn. I don't have time to do it now. I want to go to Brittany's house tonight. I'm going to walk there."

Meg's voice escalated. "You will *not* leave this house. It's dangerous to walk to Brittany's. Go to your room. You're grounded for two weeks."

Hannah stomped upstairs, slammed the door hard and sulked. Hannah used a penknife to scratch in the back of the door, "I hate mom."

When Meg discovered the door, she said, "I'm taking your iPod for a

---

I hate you

Those three words, *I hate you,* burn a parent's soul. Adopted and step-children have another way to say it: "You're not my real mother/father."

"I hate you" is often a child's way to seek revenge. "You hurt me so I'll hurt you back by withholding my love."

"I hate you" could mean a child doesn't like a limit you've set.

"I hate you" could mean you have said or done something they don't like and you don't care whether they like it or not.

When a child is hurting, parents must separate from their hurt, accept the child unconditionally and use encouragement.

Youngsters only say "I hate you" when they feel safe to say it to you, or when they are feeling younger than their age, tired, angry and/or disempowered

"I hate you" can have many meanings.

If your child regularly uses "I hate you" as a weapon, reflect on your feelings and response at the time. Do you give in and give them what they want? Do you try to hurt them back? Do you feel guilty or angry?

Have you been ignoring their pleas for attention? Are revenge or misbehavior the only ways they can get your attention? "I hate you" could be a plea for more attention.

"I hate you," could mean the child was angry and wanted to have her way. When was the last time you held a family meeting, spent some open-ended fun time with her or encouraged her?

Sometimes the best response is, "You may feel angry towards me now, and I still love you."

---

week and you're grounded for another week."

The power struggle had escalated to the point where Hannah felt discouraged and lived "down" to her mother's expectations. Meg's additional punishment reinforced Hannah's negative self-image, and fueled her resistance. Hannah threw the last punch: revenge, and conveyed the message, "You hurt me, I'll hurt you back."

When a child has progressed from needing attention, to power and seeking revenge, they are discouraged and need encouragement.

Parents must show compassion, take a step back from the situation and find the maturity to encourage the child. Parents must rise above feeling hurt and the temptation to hurt the child back.

Encouraging a child, not praising her, will enable her to reconnect to her self-worth. The more discouraged the child feels, the more love, acceptance, encouragement and consistent boundaries the child needs. Ironically, when the child acts the worst she most needs positive input, when it is hardest to give. It is imperative to encourage children at that moment.

Avoid the fracas

To steer clear of the dances of power and revenge, parents must be able to see the dance coming. One clue is for parents to observe their emotions when youngsters act out, then consciously decline to dance.

Meg could have sidestepped the situation in advance by having a family meeting to democratically allocate the chores, establish a time frame for completion, and give Hannah choices and consequences for not living up to the agreement.

It is up to the parents to follow through in a firm and friendly way. Meg can change her response to Hannah. One friendly reminder the night before or in the morning is sufficient, such as "You promised to have the lawn mowed by tomorrow night, Hannah."

Meg must refrain from nagging and threatening on Saturday. Instead, she can plan, even rehearse, a low-key response if Hannah procrastinates. The most powerful teaching will be when Mom allows Hannah to decide when and if to mow the lawn, and to experience the consequences.

By Saturday evening if Hannah hasn't mowed the lawn and asks for a ride, Meg is ready with a positive parenting plan: "I see you decided not to mow the lawn today."

Meg must anticipate that the situation may get worse before it gets better. Hannah may yell, shout accusations and seek revenge.

"I'll mow it tomorrow, I promise! Give me a ride to Brittany's house."

"Hannah, you agreed to mow the lawn by today. I will give you a ride when you do what you promised," Meg can say and leave the room. The fewer words the better. Hannah may follow Meg and yell, "Then I'll walk there or get a ride from Brittany's mother."

"No, you will not be going anywhere until the lawn is mowed." There is no need to take away her iPod or ground Hannah. One night of not getting what she wants will suffice.

"That is *so* unfair! I hate you!"

Best Foot Forward

Some might say that my first job was working at a department store in high school, but I have always thought of "shoeshine girl" as my first job. As a kid in the 1980s, I was expected to help with dusting and dishes. My special responsibility was making sure my Dad's shoes were polished, and Mom's leather heels shined.

It was presented to me as my contribution to my family, to support my parents in their work. Did I enjoy the cleaning, polishing, buffing of the shoes and shining of the bottoms of all of those loafers? No, not while I was doing it, but I felt a sense of pride and satisfaction when I was done.

Today, I run a concierge business and do everything from paying household bills, running errands, party planning, pet-sitting, to managing a pool installation or a home remodeling project.

I give people more time to focus on what they value. My life's work relates to how my parents made me feel that I had an important role in the family.

Christie Gaderson   Austin, Texas
www.prioritiesconcierge.com

When parents change their response to a youngster's behavior, the youngster may push back, harder, desperately seeking the normal route to get their way. Remember the broken vending machine: when it doesn't give you what you expect, you shake it, scream and protest.

Goal 4: Inadequacy

Diagnosed with ADD, Mike, 9, and was in the lowest groups for reading and math at school. Mike resisted getting ready for school, refused to do homework and often said, "I hate school."

During a parent-teacher conference, his teacher asked, "Does Mike have any chores at home?"

His mother responded, "It's all I can do to get him to go to school and try to get him to do homework. He never wants to do anything I suggest. There's no way I can get him to do anything that's not fun. I've given up."

Mike was desperate for a steady diet of encouragement to rebuild his self-esteem. When the child and parents have given up, the situation seems hopeless. They may benefit from professional help.

Don't confuse a child who is deeply discouraged with passive-aggressive behavior. The passive-aggressive child is waiting in the wings to seek revenge against a dominant parent. He may also be depressed and need therapy.

If a child is deeply discouraged and has convinced parents and teachers not to expect anything from him, adults must accept the child where he is and start practicing encouragement daily. Allow three to four weeks of sincere daily encouragement before expecting a change. The younger the child, the faster he will respond.

Birth order

The influence of a person's birth order and number of siblings has been well studied. Understanding the influence of birth order can explain some of children's behavior. Every birth position offers advantages and disadvantages.

Some children abdicate the traditional roles, others embrace them. Carla, the oldest of ten children in a religious family, refused to be her mother's helper and did not act like a firstborn.

In another big family, Lily served as a loyal assistant and helped her mother rear seven younger siblings. Lily learned how to manage people and projects and how to cook and sew, which benefited her throughout her life.

The biggest hazard to avoid is labeling children, no matter what their family birth order, as the smart one, the baby, the athlete, the artist, the free spirit or you-name-it.

Youngsters absorb negative and positive expectations whether said aloud or by inferred. Youths will live up or down to parental expectations.

"I don't ever expect Levi to be able to support himself," Martha whispers to friends about her son Levi, 21, an artist. Levi has taken full advantage of that unspoken belief and moved back into his parents' small home. With that whispered expectation and Martha unconsciously supporting it, Levi may never live independently.

Our culture has a variety of labels and expectations that negatively influence their development and influence young people.

"Girls are easier to raise than boys," and "Boys are easier than girls."

"Boys will be boys."

"Kate is my athlete. Liz is the artist."

"Every male in my family for the past three generations has had substance abuse problems. I'm afraid Abdul will, too."

"Ashanti is shy."

"You'll never amount to anything."

"Deepak is the baby. Everyone takes care of him. He can't even find food to eat. I have to feed him when I get home." Deepak is 17.

Any of these expectations spoken or inferred, can have a long-term impact on the child's self-view. Watch what you say, and craft open-ended positive expectations that don't limit them, or saddle youngsters with a negative family legacy.

Early self-discipline reaps rewards

I emptied the dishwasher at every night starting at age 6. I hated that simple task, even though it made things easier for my mother who turned out dinner in thirty minutes after working all day at *The Bootery*, a shoe store my parents owned in Asheville, N.C.

My more memorable job was in the store, where I was expected to work. When I was 7, my uncle challenged me to learn to count back change. It started as a game, but proved a valued skill. I remember running between my parents' store to my uncle's Army-Navy store next door, and kibitzing with sales clerks.

In 1965, when I was 12, the stores merged to form an Eddie-Bauer type store called *The Star Bootery,* which sold an array of items from dancewear to cowboy attire. I spent most Saturdays and school holidays at the store as a pre-teen and teen. I waited on customers -- remember when clerks got shoes from the storeroom and put them on customers' feet? I checked-in shipments, stocked shelves and more on Saturdays and in the summer. I got paid about $10 a week.

I often hated working in the store because other kids didn't have to because their parents didn't have stores. I felt jealous of the store because it took all my parents' time, so I swore I'd never work in it.

After earning a master's degree in folklore in 1978, I couldn't find work in documenting American culture, so I ended up managing a new store, *A Dancer's Place*, for twelve years.

By 1971, my dad had lost enthusiasm for the business and my uncle died, so my mother ran the family business from 1971 until she retired. My experience has served me well. I'm thorough and detail-oriented. I do not consider work to be a nine-to-five-thing cushioned with water-cooler talk. Growing up at the store sparked my interest in other Jewish family-owned businesses in Asheville, N.C. I discovered more than 450 existed between 1880 and 1990, which I documented in a project. www.history-at-hand.com

Jan Schochet   Chapel Hill, North Carolina
Writer, documentarian and producer--www.webtopiamarketing.com

Name it and tame it

When children misbehave, ask yourself, "What is their mistaken goal?" A clue is how you feel when the youngster is misbehaving. To change the situation, ask, "How is my response to them perpetuating the situation?" "What can I do differently?"

We cannot change others. We can only change our *response* to others. The chart on page 235 summarizes the four goals of misbehavior from Adler and Dreikurs, and expressed by Don Dinkmeyer and Gary D. MacKay in *Systematic Training for Effective Parenting.*

When you become conscious of a behavior pattern and *name it*, it becomes easier to *tame it*, and develop a different response to it. Parents must be accountable for their role in the family dynamic. It's nearly impossible to "fix" children while parents stay static. Parents must wake up to how their behavior perpetuates self-defeating behavior.

If you can name it, you can tame it. Make it a practice to regularly give positive attention, fresh, crisp potato chips, to children, to avoid them resorting to the mistaken goals of behavior.

New practice: Identify the four mistaken goals of behavior in your children and be accountable for how your responses to feeds into the situations

Challenge: Choose *one* chronic situation with one of your children and pledge to respond differently to it for three weeks. View yourself and your children like actors. Write a new script and be prepared to do the unexpected.

For discussion or journaling: How did it feel to respond differently when your child invited you to "dance" with one of the mistaken goals? What do you need to develop in yourself to internalize the new response?

Child's faulty belief		Parent's response to the misbehaving child	Child's response to parent	Positive Parenting Plan
I belong only when I'm the center of attention or when my parents are in service to me.	Attention	**Feeling:** Annoyed. **Behavior:** Nag, coax, bargain, inappropriately use logic or befriend child.	Temporarily ceases attention-getting actions. Repeats it later, or causes other disturbance.	Pay attention to children at neutral times. **Encourage.** Ignore misbehavior when possible. Avoid giving in, nagging, rewarding or punishment.
I belong only when I dominate others and prove that no one is the boss of me.	Power	**Feeling:** Threatened, angry. **Behavior:** fight back and overpower, punish, surrender.	Active and passive bids for power get stronger; child may submit to someone bigger and stronger.	**Give choices.** Decline child's invitation to spar for power. Sparring or giving in will fuel child's power drive. Engage child's help positively.
I belong only when I hurt others because I feel hurt. I am unlovable.	Revenge	**Feeling:** Hurt. **Behavior:** seek revenge on the child by hurting them back.	Behave gets worse and/or finds another strategy to hurt the parent/step-parent more.	**Choose not to feel hurt,** or seek revenge. **Do not** punish the child. **Encourage** the child daily. Love unconditionally. Build trust.
I belong only when I am helpless; others wait on me and feel sorry for me. I've given up.	Inadequacy	**Feeling:** powerless, hopeless, and desperate. **Behavior:** Agree with the child. Give up.	No change.	Begin **encouraging** the smallest efforts regularly. Do not feel sorry or give up on the child. **Have faith.**

All work and no play make Jack a dull boy.
All play and no work make Jack a mere toy.
Nursery rhyme

18

A Stalwart
Positive Parenting Plan

L ike most mothers, I loved my children and dedicated myself to
being the best mother possible.

Like many mothers, my efforts were undermined by anger, lack
of patience and lack of a plan. I hated myself when I lost my temper and
said and did things I later regretted. I mistakenly believed the children had
to suffer to learn and it was my job to punish them. Then I found the
Adlerian method and changed my approach.

It did not eliminate mistakes. I learned to have the courage to be
imperfect, learn from mistakes and be ready the next time with a positive
parenting plan. At every stage, my children showed me how to have
patience when they made not-so-good decisions. I learned to create peace
in my home and heart, and established the foundation to a lifelong
relationship with my offspring that carried us through adolescence.

I hope this book has given you the same gift. I hope you have transformed how you relate to yourself and your children. Your positive parenting plan can influence their behavior with kindness, firmness and mutual respect. It can make a big difference in you, your family and your children.

We have been given freedom of choice, and with it comes responsibility. A simple system of childhood chores is a powerful way to teach self-discipline, which can influence a child's work habits for life.

Responsible people are more likely to make and keep commitments in life in school, at work, to people, to a spouse and family, to their community and country. I want to be able to count on people to do what they say they're going to do, even if they don't like it or it's inconvenient. Chores teach that kind of responsibility and work ethic.

It's critical to use a velvet glove to motivate children to do chores in order to avoid breeding resentment and revenge. Chores, responsibility and a work ethic don't come naturally because humans choose the easiest path.

Parents must motivate children kindly and firmly to contribute without the manipulation of money or threat of punishment. That's where the other Adlerian techniques come in: holding family meetings, showing mutual respect, using encouragement, giving choices and using natural and logical consequences. As you have learned, these are the basics of a **positive parenting plan.**

It takes time and energy to enlist the help of your family members around the house so you can retire from being the house servant. Even though their efforts may never live up to your standards, it is worthwhile to involve them in maintaining your home.

Doing chores will have long-term payoffs, like this 49-year-old woman wrote in my survey. "I truly learned a lot as I did chores that I now use to make my life easier today. How to remove stains in our laundry, how to cook for large groups on a budget from scratch, how to have fun while pitching in, and the old adage *many hands make light work.* I look back and realize how much I learned as I was growing up, what I thought as hard were things that other friends never learned, how to iron a shirt, fold linens, set a proper table, all sorts of things I never thought I would use in life."

What happened to your most pressing problem?

What is different since writing down your most pressing problem? How did your positive parenting plan change your thoughts, feelings and actions that in turn, influenced your children to make new choices?

The most valuable payoff for a positive parenting plan is its long-term nature. Changing how you respond to your children sets a calm, democratic tone that minimizes criticism, nagging, punishment, reward and praise.

Having one consistent positive parenting plan is a rudder in calm and crazy weather. Children and teens thrive on routine, fairness and mutual respect.

By implementing the strategies presented in this book, I predict your most pressing problem has diminished dramatically. You have learned a variety of techniques to change your responses and get different results.

60 miles away going 60 miles an hour

Having lived with multiple teens for thirteen years, my goal for them was simple: that they make good independent decisions when I'm 60 miles away and they're going 60 miles an hour.

I want them to be sober, in a seatbelt and use a condom every time. That covers many basic safety rules of life.

My children got practice making decisions when they were held responsible for chores, given freedom to manage their school life and kept their bedrooms however they wanted. When they reached adolescence they were prepared to live with the outcome of their choices.

For many readers, the teen years are far away, so I hope you will lay the foundation now for an adolescence filled with mutual respect and good decision-making. Be stalwart and maintain a vision. If you change your behavior with 100 percent conviction, your offspring will change their response to you.

Continuing education

Real change takes time. Reading books and raising awareness takes time. If you are committed to creating different results, stick to this new path. Network with other parents and read other Adlerian books together.

Ask your local school or community center to lead a study group for parents. Sign up for my online course, and take it more than once. Learn from your mistakes. Take it easy on yourself. Have the courage to be imperfect, to be a good-enough parent. There are no perfect parents, children or families.

To quote a coaching client, "normal" is a cycle on the dryer.

Stay in touch

Check my blog **www.raisingable.com,** for updates. I welcome comments about your successes and challenges. I'm especially interested in the results of how your family implements chores.

A positive parenting approach can be learned by reading this book. To recondition your responses to family members, anticipate at least three months, plus follow up, such as taking refresher courses twice a year. Allow two to three years of study and practice for a total transformation. Make a commitment to a positive parenting plan for the sake of yourself, your marriage and your family, in that order.

The years will fly by. In hindsight, the challenges of young children will shrink in magnitude when compared to those of tweens and teens. Enjoy the present moment with your children. Have fun with the family meetings, dinner and work sessions because they will soon be sealed in the time capsule of childhood.

The basics of a positive parenting plan

Many families and schools have adopted the following thirty-four practices summarized in *Children: The Challenge* by Dreikurs and Soltz.

Encourage the child.

Avoid punishment and reward.

Use natural and logical consequences.

Be firm without dominating.

Respect the child.

Induce respect for order.

Induce respect for the rights of others.

Eliminate criticism and minimize mistakes.

Maintain routine.

Take time for training.

Win co-operation.

Avoid giving undue attention.

Sidestep the struggle for power.

Withdraw from the conflict.

Act! Keep your mouth shut.

Don't shoo flies.

Use care in pleasing – have the courage to say "No."

Avoid that first impulse – do the unexpected.

Refrain from overprotection.

Stimulate independence.

Stay out of fights.

Be unimpressed by fears.

Mind your own business.

Avoid the pitfalls of pity.

Make requests reasonable and sparse.

Follow through – be consistent.

Put them all in the same boat.

Listen!

Watch your tone of voice.

Take it easy.

Downgrade "bad" habits.

Have fun together.

Talk with *them,* not *to* them.

Establish a family council (family meeting).

Acknowledgments

This book was made possible because of my husband "Reliable" Bob Williams. *Without you, everything would be different. With you, my life is everything I dreamed.* Casey, Noah, Ian and Kristen, I appreciate the countless gifts you have shared, especially acceptance, patience, stalwartness, creativity and humor.

Thanks to: participants in my parenting workshops and coaching clients; my Mastermind Group -- Dennis Mahoney, Duane LeFevere, Belinda Fuchs and Elizabeth Freedman; my incredible coach Joe Stallone; Bev Stohl and the Totem Mamas -- Shelley Hartz, Laura Gimby and Jan Duston; and Ray Glazier and Abt Associates for interpreting the survey data.

Thanks to my family -- my parents Mildred and John, Jim, Kathy, Jean, Paul, Stephen, Danny Mary, Brian, and the rest of the Tordella clan; my community at First Church Unitarian in Littleton, Massachusetts; Dean and friends at The Bridge Spot; Renaissance Advanced Toastmasters Club; the 564 people who took my survey; and people who contributed wonderful stories through HARO (Help Out A Reporter).

Thanks to individuals who contributed interviews and experiences including Jamie Bafundo, Peter Bosch, Barbara Caldwell-Miller, Bernadett Campbell, Vivian Chen, Sarah Chandler, Catherine Dolan-Haas, Denali Delmar, Deb Farrand, Derek Devenne, Michelle Drollet, Helen Lemoine, Lisa Masure, Mike Mintz, Mike O'Neill, Jane Nelsen, Charlie Parsons, Kendra Pennington, Cliff Ryding, Kathleen Sylvia, Paul Tordella, Sarah Watson, Emily Welch, John Wendell, Dave and Sandy Williams, Zoe Williams, Arnie Zide and others.

Thanks to Denali Delmar, Shelley Hartz, Carol Sheingold, and Casey Williams for editorial assistance.

Last but not least, thanks to an editor who en**courage**d me to keep climbing when the mountain seemed impossibly steep, Bill Wooley.

About the Author

Born and raised in Wilmington, Delaware as the eighth of nine children, Susan Tordella married Bob Williams at age 22 and started a family immediately. When many of her peers were dressing for success, Susan had four children in seven years.

While a domo-guru, Susan taught parenting skills workshops. She said, "My best teaching tool was to share my mistakes so other parents were free to share theirs and we could learn from them. *Perfect* describes diamonds, not parents."

With three teens at home, Susan took a paid job as a reporter, and then became editor of the Littleton Independent. Susan supported Bob's transition from a corporate job to establishing a successful business as a home renovations contractor. As director of a private-non-profit, Susan promoted carpooling, biking taking public transit and walking to work to employees of Fortune 500 companies.

Susan divides her time as a writer, parenting coach and workshop leader, speaker, and volunteer. Susan has co-founded several Toastmasters clubs for prison inmates to build confidence, public speaking and leadership skills.

"The refrain I hear from inmates is, 'I made some bad decisions.' That's the goal of raising capable children: to nurture them to make good decisions when they're 60 miles away, going 60 miles an hour," she said.

Watch for Susan's next books, **Choose Well** *when you're 60 miles away going 60 miles an hour*, for parents of teenagers and **Great Expectations: How to grow children to eat vegetables.**

Sources

Chapter 1

Dreikurs, Rudolf M.D. with Soltz, Vicki R.N. *Children: the Challenge.* New York: Plume, an imprint of New American Library, Penguin Books USA Inc. Copyright 1964, reissued in 1987 by E.P. Dutton.

www.Wikipedia.com. List of Latin words with English derivatives.

Chapter 3

Dreikurs, Rudolf M.D. with Soltz, Vicki R.N. *Children: the Challenge.*

Lott, Lynn and Intner, Riki. *Chores without Wars: Turning housework into teamwork.* Lanham, Md.: Taylor Trade Publishing. Copyright 2005 by Lynn Lott and Riki Intner.

"What is a Mom Worth? Working mom vs. Stay at Home Mom Salaries for 2006." http://www.salary.com/aboutus/layoutscripts/abtl_default.asp?tab=abt&cat=cat012&ser=ser041&part=Par481

Chapter 4

Branden, Nathaniel. *Honoring the Self.* Los Angeles: Bantam Books and Jeremy P. Tarcher, Inc. Copyright 1983 by Nathaniel Branden.

Jones, Nancy P., "BIG JOBS: Planning for Competence." Reprinted with permission from Young Children. Washington: March 2005. Vol. 60, Issue 2; Pages 86-94. http://www.childrensfarm.org/index.html.

Nelsen, Jane, Ph.D. *Positive Discipline.* New York: Ballantine Books. Copyright 1981, 1987 by Jane Nelsen. www.positivediscipline.com.

Chapter 5

Levine, Madeline, Ph.D. *The Price of Privilege.* New York: Harper Collins. Copyright 2006 by Madeline Levine, Ph.D.

Mahler, Jonathan. "James Patterson Inc.," New York Times, Jan. 20, 2010. http://www.nytimes.com/2010/01/24/magazine/24patterson-t.html?ref=books&pagewanted=all.

Nelsen, Jane, Ph.D. *Positive Discipline.*

Chapter 7

Branden, Nathaniel. *Honoring the Self.*

Dreikurs, Rudolf M.D. with Soltz, Vicki R.N. *Children: the Challenge.*

Myers, David G. Ph.D. *The Pursuit of Happiness, Who is Happy and Why.* New York: William Morrow and Co. Copyright 1992 by David G. and Carol P. Myers Charitable Foundation

Nelsen, Jane, Ph.D. *Positive Discipline.*

Chapter 9

"Be Prepared," an interview with Baden-Powell by the "Listener" magazine in 1937 http://www.pinetreeweb.com/bp-listener.htm.

Lott, Lynn and Intner, Riki. *Chores without Wars: turning housework into teamwork.*

Tolle, Eckhart. *The Art of Presence.* Sound recording. Boulder, Col.: Sounds True. Copyright 2007 by Eckhart Teachings.

Chapter 10

Anderson, Sarah, Ph.D., Whitaker, Robert, M.D., M.P.H. "Household Routines and Obesity in US Preschool-Aged Children" in Pediatrics, Vol. 125 No. 3 March 2010, pp. 420-428.

CASA, The National Center on Addiction and Substance Abuse at Columbia University. "The Importance of Family Dinners IV." http://www.casacolumbia.org/articlefiles/380importance%20of%20Family%20Dinners%20IV.pdf. Sept. 2007.

Nelsen, Jane, Ph.D. *Positive Discipline.*

Chapter 11

Bergstrom, Jan, M.A. Marriage counselor. www.janbergstrom.com.

Twenge, Jean Ph.D. *Generation Me.* New York: Free Press, a division of Simon & Schuster. Copyright 2006 by Jean M. Twenge, Ph.D.

Chapter 12

Branden, Nathaniel. *Honoring the Self.*

Burr, Wesley R. and Christensen, Clark. "Undesirable Side Effects of Enhancing Self-esteem," in National Council Family Relations, Vol. 41, No. 4, Oct. 1992, pp. 460-464.

Myers, David G. Ph.D. *The Pursuit of Happiness, Who is Happy and Why.*

Twenge, Jean Ph.D. *Generation Me.*

Chapter 13

Linden, Larry. http://careergamechampionships.com.

Thich Nhat Hanh. *Peace is Every Step.* New York: Bantam Doubleday Dell Publishing Group. Copyright 1991 by Thich Nhat Hanh.

Chapter 14

2008 National Household Travel Survey
http://www.walktoschool.org/resources/talking-points.cfm
http://www.cdc.gov/nchs/data/nvsr/nvsr57/nvsr57_14.pdf

Gershon, David. *The Low Carbon Diet.* Woodstock, N.Y.: The Empowerment Institute. Copyright 2006 by David Gershon.

Skenazy, Lenore. *Free Range Kids.* San Francisco: Jossey-Bass, a Wiley Imprint. Copyright 2009 by Lenore Skenazy.

Chapter 15

Linn, Susan. *The Case for Make Believe.* New York: New Press, distributed by W.W. Norton & Co., Inc. Copyright 2008 by Susan Linn.

Chapter 17

Adler, Alfred, MD. *Understanding Human Nature,* translated by Colin Brett. New York: Greenberg. Copyright 1939 and 1992, by One World Publications Ltd. Originally published in German in 1927.

Dinkmeyer, Don and McKay, Gary D. *The Parents Handbook – Systematic Training for Effective Parenting.* Circle Pines, Minn.: American Guidance Service. Copyright 1989 AGS. First edition copyright 1976.

Dreikurs, Rudolf M.D. with Soltz, Vicki R.N. *Children: the Challenge.*

Index